A Box of Delights

A BOX of Delights

J. John
and
Mark Stibbe

MONARCH
BOOKS
OXFORD, UK, & GRAND RAPIDS, MICHIGAN

First published in the UK in 2001 by Monarch Books,
(a publishing imprint of Lion Hudson plc),
Mayfield House, 256 Banbury Road, Oxford OX2 7DH.
Tel: +44 (0) 1865 302750 Fax: +44 (0) 1865 302757
Email: monarch@lionhudson.com
www.lionhudson.com
Reprinted 2002 (twice), 2003, 2004, 2006.

Published in the USA in 2002 by Monarch Books.

Illustrations by Darren Harvey Regan.

Distributed by:
UK: Marston Book Services Ltd, PO Box 269, Abingdon, Oxon OX14 4YN;
USA: Kregel Publications, PO Box 2607 Grand Rapids, Michigan 49501.

ISBN-10: 1 85424 547 3 (UK)
ISBN-13: 978 1 85424 547 2 (UK)
ISBN-10: 0 8254 6027 1 (USA)
ISBN-13: 978 0 8254 6027 2 (USA)

British Library Cataloguing Data
A catalogue record for this book is available
from the British Library.

Printed and bound in Malta by Gutenberg Press.

Acknowledgements

Our thanks to those who have given us permission to use material reproduced in this collection. Every effort has been made to trace the original copyright holders where required. In some cases this has proved impossible. We shall be happy to correct any such omissions in future editions.

Note to church magazine editors

Introduction

Go onto the streets today and ask people what the word 'church' means to them and they will almost always reply 'boring'.

It's one of the saddest facts of life that a church service is regarded by most contemporary people as an hour and a half of unmitigated tedium. And that's just by those who already go. Those who don't go to church either have distant memories of sitting through a service, or they have heard on the cultural grapevine that this is the case.

When Johnathan Stibbe was about three years old, he made up a song and sang it frequently round the house. The refrain went, 'God's not boring.'

How absolutely true! God isn't boring. He's the most interesting, relevant and understanding person in the universe. It's the church that's the problem, not God.

Right at the top of the list of those responsible is of course the preacher. Preaching today is definitely a lost art. There are many reasons for this, not least the fact that most of those called to preach are now ridiculously overworked during the week and have little time for prayer and preparation. Excuses aside, it's time to get back to the priorities of Jesus, and one of his main priorities was to communicate about the kingdom of God in a relevant way.

Everyone knows that Jesus could not only draw a crowd, he could hold their attention. He spoke in an idiom that everyone understood, and he told brief stories that grabbed people. Before they knew it, his listeners were caught in a net of uncompromising truths that directly challenged their values and priorities. The hills of Galilee were his pulpit and his everyday surroundings were his subject matter. In short, his teaching was colourful.

The two things Jesus used more than anything else were parables and proverbs. Parables are earthly stories that illustrate heavenly truths. Proverbs are terse sayings that express in a simple way the deep wisdom of the kingdom of God.

In this book we have pooled nearly forty years' worth of preaching experience to give away a stock of our best parables and proverbs. We have only included items that are short and that actually work in practice. We hope that they will greatly increase your effectiveness as a communicator.

In the end, however, both of us want to say that you can have the best parables and proverbs in the world, but if you do not have God's power, all this is of little use. We need God's anointing and God's help in both the preparation and delivery of the message. The following little exchange between a preacher and his daughter highlights the issue:

Daughter: Daddy, why do you close your eyes and bow your head for a moment before you give the sermon?
Daddy: Because, my dear, I'm asking God for help.
Daughter: Then why doesn't he?

We need divine resources as well as human ones.

In our School of Preaching training days, we have often referred to the story of DL Moody's transformation as a preacher. In a sermon entitled 'Why God used DL Moody', RA Torrey told this story:

In his early days Moody was a great hustler; he had a tremendous desire to do something, but he had no real power. He worked very largely in the energy of the flesh. But there were two humble Free Methodist women who used to come over to his meetings in the YMCA. One was 'Auntie Cook' and the other, Mrs Snow. (I think her name was not Snow at that time.) These two women would come to Mr Moody at the close of his meetings and say: 'We are praying for you.' Finally, Mr Moody became somewhat nettled and said to them one night: 'Why are you praying for me? Why don't you pray for the unsaved?' They replied: 'We are praying that you may get the power.'

Not long after, one day on his way to England, he was walking up Wall Street in New York; and in the midst of the bustle and hurry of that city his prayer was answered; the power of God fell upon him as he walked up the street. He went out with the power of the Holy Ghost upon him, and when he got to London, the power of God wrought through him mightily in North London, and hundreds were added to the churches.

From this moment on, Moody was powerfully used by God. Where twenty or thirty people had responded to his preaching before, now ten times that number responded. The anointing of the Holy Spirit made the difference.

And so we need the power of God not just the resources of men and women. This book, we pray, will help. But there is something not provided in this volume that we all constantly need to seek: the power of the Holy Spirit. As Jesus said in his first sermon, quoting the prophet Isaiah, 'The Spirit of the sovereign Lord is upon me and has anointed me to preach good news to the poor' (Luke 4.18).

May God increase his anointing in the lives of all of those who are called to communicate the truths of the kingdom.

J. John and Mark Stibbe

Adoption

A class of junior school children were discussing a picture of a family. One little boy in the picture had different colour hair from the other family members in the picture. One child suggested that he was adopted and a little girl said, 'I know all about adoptions because I was adopted.'

'What does it mean to be adopted?' asked another child.

'It means,' said the girl, 'that you grew in your mummy's heart instead of her tummy.'

In New Zealand, a country known for its sheep industry, during the yearly lambing season, thousands of baby lambs are born. Unfortunately, some lambs die at birth. Many mother sheep also die giving birth.

In an attempt to save the orphaned lambs, the shepherds match baby lambs who have lost their mothers with mother sheep who have lost their lambs. But a mother sheep won't accept a lamb and nurse it unless it is her own.

How, then, do shepherds get a mother sheep to accept an orphan lamb as her own? The process is as old as shepherding itself. The mother's own lamb, which has died, is skinned and the skin of the dead lamb is draped over the living lamb as it is placed by the adoptive mother's side. The mother sheep then smells the skin and accepts the orphaned lamb as her own.

Age

I finally got my head together. Now my body's falling apart.

One cannot help being old, but one can resist being aged.

'The most aggravating thing about the younger generation is that I no longer belong to it.'

Albert Einstein

There's many a good tune on an old fiddle.

When you're over the hill you pick up speed.

Alcohol

A preacher was completing a temperance sermon: with great expression he said, 'If I had all the beer in the world, I'd take it and throw it into the river.'

With even greater emphasis he said, 'And if I had all the wine in the world, I'd take it and throw it into the river.'

And then finally, he said, 'And if I had all the whisky in the world, I'd take it and throw it into the river.'

He sat down. The song leader then stood very cautiously and announced with a smile, 'For our closing song, let us sing Hymn 365: "Shall We Gather at the River?".'

Anglicans

A father took his son to an Anglican church. They normally attended a Congregational church where there wasn't much participation by the children, but the children could all say the Lord's Prayer together. When the Lord's Prayer was said in the Congregational church the little boy would stand on the pew and loudly go through the Lord's Prayer. When they were in the Anglican church they got to the Lord's Prayer and the little boy stood on the pew and as loud as he could began to recite the Lord's Prayer. But in this Anglican church they stopped after 'Lead us not into temptation, but deliver us from evil....', but the little boy then went on still loudly saying, 'For thine is the kingdom, the power....' on his own and then realised that he was the only one speaking. He turned to his daddy and said, 'Daddy, there's no power and glory in this church.'

Apathy

I wonder what troubles God the most, lost sinners stumbling through a cold dark night, or carefree saints sleeping in his bright warm light.

Appearances

There's a story about a security guard at a factory. One day this guard stopped a worker who was walking out of the factory gate, pushing a wheelbarrow with a suspicious-looking package in it. The guard opened up the package to find that it contained nothing but some old bits of rubbish, sawdust and sweepings from the floor.

The next day he stopped the same worker who once again was pushing a wheelbarrow containing a suspicious-looking package. Once more it contained nothing of value.

After the same thing had happened many days in succession, the guard finally said to the worker, 'OK, I give up. I know you must be up to something but I don't know what it is. I promise I won't arrest you, but please put me out of my misery. Tell me what you are stealing.'

The worker looked at the guard and smiled as he replied, 'Wheelbarrows, my friend, I'm stealing wheelbarrows.'

Some Christians give the impression they have been baptised in vinegar!

There's a face-lift you can perform yourself that is guaranteed to improve your appearance. It's called a smile.

Assurance

A priest was preparing a dying man for his long day's journey into night.

Whispering firmly, the priest said, 'Denounce the devil! Let him know how little you think of his evil!'

The dying man said nothing.

The priest repeated his order. Still the dying man said nothing.

The priest asked, 'Why do you refuse to denounce the devil and his evil?'

The dying man said, 'Until I know where I'm heading, I don't think I ought to aggravate anybody!'

Atheism

An atheist was spending a quiet day fishing when suddenly his boat was attacked by the Loch Ness monster. In one easy flip, the beast tossed him and his boat high into the air. Then it opened its mouth to swallow both.

As the man sailed head over heels, he cried out, 'Oh, my God! Help me!'

At once, the ferocious attack scene froze in place, and as the atheist hung in mid-air, a booming voice came down from the clouds, 'I thought you didn't believe in me!'

'Come on God, give me a break!' the man pleaded. 'Two minutes ago I didn't believe in the Loch Ness monster either!'

 An atheist hopes God will do nothing to disturb his disbelief.

A young woman teacher with obvious liberal tendencies explains to her class of small children that she is an atheist. She asks her class if they are atheists too. Not really knowing what atheism is but wanting to be like their teacher, their hands shoot into the air. There is, however, one exception. A beautiful girl named Lucy has not gone along with the crowd. The teacher asks her why she has decided to be different.

'Because I'm not an atheist.'

'Then,' asks the teacher, 'what are you?'

'I'm a Christian.'

The teacher is a little perturbed now, her face slightly red. She asks Lucy why she is a Christian.

'Well, I was brought up knowing and loving Jesus. My mum is a Christian, and my dad is a Christian, I also accepted Christ as my personal saviour and I am a Christian.'

The teacher is now angry.

'That's no reason,' she says loudly. 'What if your mum had been a moron, and your dad had been a moron. What would you be then?'

After a pause, and a smile.

'Then,' says Lucy, 'I'd be an atheist.'

B

Bereavement

'An odd by-product of my loss is that I am aware of being an embarrassment to everyone I meet, at work, at the club, in the street. I see people as they approach me trying to make up their minds whether they will say something about it or not. I hate it if they do and hate it if they don't. Some avoid it altogether. I like best the well brought-up young men who walk up to me as if I were a dentist, turn very red, get it over and then edge away to the bar as quickly as they decently can. Perhaps the bereaved ought to be isolated in special settlements like lepers.'

CS Lewis, writing after the death of his wife.

Bible

'You Christians look after a document containing enough dynamite to blow all civilisation to pieces, turn the world upside down, and bring peace to a battle-torn planet. But you treat it as though it is nothing more than a piece of literature.'

Mahatma Ghandi

The Bible contains the vitamins for a healthy soul.

Dusty Bibles make for dirty lives.

'I am a creature of a day, passing through life as an arrow through the air. A few moments hence, I am no more seen — I drop into eternity. I want to know one thing. The way to heaven. God has given us a way, written in the Good Book, the Bible. O give me that book! At any price, give me the book of God!'

John Wesley

A Christian lady surprised a burglar in her kitchen. He was all loaded down with the things he was going to steal. She had no weapon and was all alone. The only thing that she could think of doing was to quote Scripture. So, she held up a hand and said, 'Acts 2:38!'

The burglar quaked in fear and then froze to the point that she was able to get to the phone and call for the police.

When the police arrived, the burglar was still frozen in place. They were very much surprised that a woman alone with no weapon could do this.

One of them asked the lady, 'How did you do this?'

The woman replied, 'I quoted Scripture.'

The officer turned to the burglar, 'What was it about the scripture that had such an effect on you?'

The burglar replied, 'Scripture! What Scripture? I thought she said she had an axe and two 38s.'

A father was approached by his small son, who told him proudly, 'I know what the Bible means!'

His father smiled and replied, 'What do you mean, you "know" what the Bible means?'

The son replied, 'I do know!'

'OK,' said his father. 'So, son, what does the Bible mean?'

'That's easy, Daddy. It stands for "Basic Information Before Leaving Earth".'

The person who merely samples the word of God never acquires much of a taste for it.

'It is impossible to rightly govern the world without God and the Bible.'	**George Washington** (1732-1799), the first US President

'That Book accounts for the supremacy of England.'
Queen Victoria (1819-1901),
British monarch for sixty-four years, the longest reign in British history.

'I believe the Bible is the best gift God has ever given to man. All the good from the Saviour of the world is communicated to us through this book.'
Abraham Lincoln (1809-1865), sixteenth US President

'I have known ninety-five of the world's great men in my time, and of these, eighty-seven were followers of the Bible. The Bible is stamped with a Specialty of Origin, and an immeasurable distance separates it from all competitors.'
William Gladstone (1809-1898),
British statesman, served as Prime Minister four times.

'The Bible is the sheet-anchor of our liberties.'
Ulysses S. Grant (1822-1885), eighteenth US President

'The Bible is no mere book, but a Living Creature, with a power that conquers all that oppose it.'
Napoleon Bonaparte (1769-1821), Emperor of the French

'It is impossible to enslave mentally or socially a Bible-reading people. The principles of the Bible are the groundwork of human freedom.'
Horace Greeley (1811-1872), American newspaper editor.

'There are more sure marks of authenticity in the Bible than in any profane history.' **Sir Isaac Newton** (1642-1727), English physicist, one of the greatest scientists of all time.

'All human discoveries seem to be made only for the purpose of confirming more and more the Truths contained in the Sacred Scriptures.'
Sir William Herschel (1738-1822), English astronomer. He made numerous discoveries about the laws of the heavens.

'The Bible is the truest utterance that ever came by alphabetic letters from the soul of man, through which, as through a window divinely opened, all men can look into the stillness of eternity, and discern in glimpses their far-distant, long-forgotten home.' **Thomas Carlyle**

'Whatever merit there is in anything that I have written is simply due to the fact that when I was a child my mother daily read me a part of the Bible and daily made me learn a part of it by heart.' **John Ruskin**

'The existence of the Bible, as a book for the people, is the greatest benefit which the human race has ever experienced. Every attempt to belittle it is a crime against humanity.'
Immanuel Kant

'The New Testament is the very best book that ever was or ever will be known in the world.' **Charles Dickens**

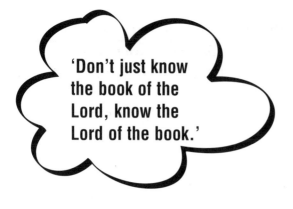

'Don't just know the book of the Lord, know the Lord of the book.'

Many Christians expect the world to respect a book that they themselves neglect.

Boldness

In 1998 a pastor by the name of Joe Wright was asked to open the new session of Kansas Senate in prayer. Instead of the politically correct prayer that everyone expected they got a passionate plea for the nation to be brought to repentance. Some of the legislators were so incensed they walked out as the pastor prayed. Here is the prayer in its entirety.

Heavenly Father, we come before you today to ask your forgiveness and seek your direction and guidance. We know your word says 'Woe to those who call evil good', but that's exactly what we have done. We have lost our spiritual equilibrium and inverted our values. We confess that. We have ridiculed the absolute truth of your word and called it pluralism. We have worshipped other gods and called it multiculturalism. We have endorsed perversion and called it an alternative lifestyle. We have exploited the poor and called it the lottery. We have neglected the needy and called it self-preservation. We have rewarded laziness and called it welfare. We have killed our unborn and called it a choice. We have shot abortionists and called it justifiable. We have neglected to discipline our children and called it building self-esteem. We have abused power and called it political savvy. We have coveted our neighbour's possessions and called it ambition. We have polluted the air with profanity and pornography and called it freedom of expression. We have ridiculed the time-honoured values of our forefathers and called it enlightenment.

Search us, O God, and know our hearts today; cleanse us from every sin and set us free. Guide and bless these men and women who have been sent here by the people of Kansas, and who have been ordained by you to govern this great state. Grant them the wisdom to rule and may their decisions direct us to the centre of your will.

I ask this in the name of your Son, the living Saviour, Jesus Christ.

Amen.

Books

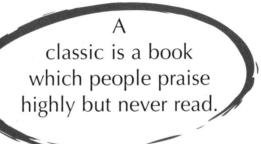

A classic is a book which people praise highly but never read.

'The best-selling books are cookbooks. The second best-selling books are dieting manuals, which teach you not to eat what you've just learnt to cook.'
Andy Rooney

Brain

 The brain is a wonderful organ. It starts working the moment you get up in the morning and does not stop until you get into the office.
Robert Frost

Brothers and sisters

A Sunday school teacher was discussing the Ten Commandments with her five and six-year-olds. After explaining the commandment to 'honour your father and your mother', she asked, 'Is there a commandment that teaches us how to treat our brothers and sisters?' Without missing a beat, one boy (the oldest of a family of seven) answered, 'Thou shalt not kill.'

Challenges

> 'The ultimate measure of a person is not where they stand in moments of comfort and convenience, but where they stand at times of challenge and controversy.'
>
> **Dr. Martin Luther King, Jr.**

Character

Brains and beauty are God's gifts; character is your own achievement.

Children

'Children have never been very good at listening to their elders, but they have never failed to imitate them.' **James Baldwin**

'The best thing to spend on your children is your time.'
Louise Hart

'Our children need our presence more than our presents.'
Jesse Jackson

'Children have more need of models than of critics.'
Joseph Joubert (1754-1824)

A father was reading Bible stories to his young son. He read, 'The man named Lot was warned to take his wife and flee out of the city, but his wife looked back and was turned to salt.' His son asked, 'What happened to the flea?'

> A four-year-old girl was learning to say the Lord's Prayer. She was reciting it all by herself without help from her mother. She said, 'And lead us not into temptation, but deliver us some e-mail. Amen.'

A four-year-old was at the paediatrician for a check up. As the doctor looked down her ears with a stethoscope, he asked, 'Do you think I'll find Big Bird in here?'

The little girl stayed silent. Next, the doctor took a tongue depressor and looked down her throat. He asked, 'Do you think I'll find the Cookie Monster down there?'

Again, the little girl was silent. Then the doctor put a stethoscope to her chest. As he listened to her heartbeat, he asked, 'Do you think I'll hear Barney in there?'

'Oh, no!' the little girl replied. 'Jesus is in my heart. Barney's on my underpants.'

During a dinner party, the hosts' two little children entered the dining room totally nude and walked slowly around the table.

The parents were so embarrassed that they pretended nothing was happening and kept the conversation going.

The guests co-operated and also continued as if nothing extraordinary was happening. After going all the way around the room, the children left.

As they disappeared out of sight, there was a moment of silence at the table, during which one child was heard to say, 'You see, it *is* vanishing cream!'

The Sunday school teacher was carefully explaining the story of Elijah the prophet and the false prophets of Baal. She explained how Elijah built the altar, put wood upon it, cut the bull in pieces and laid it upon the altar. And then Elijah commanded the people of God to fill four barrels of water and pour it over the altar. He had them do this four times.

'Now,' said the teacher, 'can anyone in the class tell me why the Lord would have Elijah pour water over the bull on the altar?'

A little girl in the back of the room raised her hand with great enthusiasm. 'To make the gravy,' came her enthusiastic reply.

Six-year-old Angie and her four-year-old brother Joel were sitting together in church. Joel giggled, sang and talked out loud. Finally, his big sister had had enough.

'You're not supposed to talk out loud in church.'

'Why? Who's going to stop me?' Joel asked.

Angie pointed to the back of the church and said,

'See those two men standing by the door? They're hushers.'

Christmas

At Christmas-time, when we receive presents we don't really need, God offers us a gift we cannot do without.

Christmas is a time when we want our past forgotten and our PRESENT remembered.

God couldn't have made himself bigger to impress us so he made himself smaller to attract us.

Don't miss Christmas. The innkeeper did because he was too preoccupied with his business. The Jewish leaders did because they couldn't be bothered to walk five miles to check things out. Herod did because he was threatened by a baby.

Have you noticed how we invest Santa Claus with the very attributes that Jesus, in the incarnation, DIVESTED himself of?

1. Omniscience. There are approximately two billion children in the world. However, since Santa does not visit children of Muslim, Hindu, Jewish or Buddhist religions, Santa knows exactly the 378 million kids to visit and their addresses. At an average rate of 3.5 children per household, that comes to 108 million homes, presuming that there is at least one good child in each.

2. Omnipresence. Santa has about 31 hours of Christmas to work with, thanks to the different time zones and the rotation of the earth, assuming he travels east to west (which seems logical). This works out to 967.7 visits per second. This is to say that for each Christian household with a good child, Santa has around 1/1000th of a second to park the sleigh, hop out, jump down the chimney, fill the stockings, distribute the remaining presents under the tree, eat whatever snacks have been left for him, get back up the chimney, jump into the sleigh and get on to the next house. Assuming that each of these 108 million stops is evenly distributed around the earth (which, of course, we know to be false), we are now talking about 0.78 miles per household; a total trip of 75.5 million miles, not counting loo breaks. This means Santa's sleigh is moving at 650 miles per second — 3,000 times the speed of sound. This accounts for how Santa can almost be everywhere at the same time!

3. Omnipotence. The payload of the sleigh adds another interesting element and highlights Santa's superhuman powers. Assuming that each child gets nothing more than a medium sized Lego set (two pounds), the sleigh is carrying over 500 thousand tons, not counting Santa himself. On land, a conventional reindeer can pull no more than 300 pounds. Even granting that the 'flying' reindeer could pull ten times the normal amount, the job can't be done with eight or even nine of them — Santa would need 360,000 of them. This increases the payload, not counting the weight of the sleigh, another 54,000 tons, or roughly seven times the weight of the Queen Elizabeth (the ship, not the monarch). 600,000 tons travelling at 650 miles per second creates enormous air resistance — this would heat up the reindeer in the same fashion as a spacecraft re-entering the earth's atmosphere. The lead pair of reindeer would absorb 14.3 quintillion joules of energy per second each. In short, they would burst into flames almost instantaneously, exposing the reindeer behind them and creating deafening sonic booms in their wake. The entire reindeer team would be vaporised within 4.26 thousandths of a second, or right about the time Santa reached the fifth house on his trip. Not that it matters, however, since Santa, as a result of accelerating from a dead stop 650 mps in .001 seconds, would be subjected to centrifugal forces of 17,500 g's. A 250 pound Santa (which seems ludicrously slim) would be pinned to the back of the sleigh by 4,315,015 pounds of force, instantly crushing his bones and organs and reducing him to a quivering blob of pink goo. Only an omnipotent Santa could achieve such a task...

Anon

A seven-year old child was drawing a picture of the nativity. The picture was very good, including Mary, Joseph and, of course, baby Jesus. However, there was a fat man standing in the corner of the stable that just did not seem to fit in. When the child was asked about it, she replied, 'Oh, that's Round John Virgin.'

If you take Christ out of Christmas, all you're left with is M & S...

Paul Wilson

I received the following message on the front of a Christmas card in 1998:

> Some people think that Christmas time
> Is gifts and grub and booze;
> But the best bit is
> That Jesus came —
> God's Son in human shoes.

A 1999 survey by television company OnDigital has found that among the under-thirties, people know more about Christmas television programmes than they do about Christmas itself. In the survey, only 28% of the age group could name the three gifts brought by the wise men to Jesus, and only one in five knew that the king who ordered the killing of the firstborn was called Herod. In contrast, 64% knew that the television detective who drove a red Jaguar was called Morse.

The average person will gain six pounds during the Christmas season. Here are guidelines for Christmas eating:

1   If you eat something and no one sees you eat it, it has no calories.

2   If you drink a diet drink with chocolate, the calories in the chocolate bar are cancelled by the diet drink.

3   When you eat with someone else calories don't count if you don't eat more than they do.

4   Drink used for medicinal purposes never counts eg. mulled wine, sherry and brandy.

5   If you fatten everyone else around you, you'll look thinner.

6   Biscuit pieces and crumbs contain no calories; the process of breaking causes calorie leakage.

7   Things licked off spoons have no calories, especially home-made brandy butter.

8   Foods with similar colouring have the same calories, ie turkey and white chocolate.

Put these words on an OHP: *cheers and applause, cheers, applause, boos, hiss, huh, cheers and boos, moan.* Ask someone to point to the relevant response on the OHP as the reading progresses. Then read out the following passage. It goes down brilliantly and is the *only* way we know of making the genealogy of Jesus interesting!

The book of the genealogy of Jesus Christ *(cheers and applause)*

The son of David *(cheers)*

The son of Abraham *(applause)*

Who pretended Sarah was his sister and let Pharaoh have her and received much cattle *(boos)*

Abraham was the father of Isaac whose name means laughter *(cheers)*

And Isaac the father of Jacob who stole his brother's birthright *(hiss)*

And Jacob was the father of Judah and his brothers who sold Joseph into slavery *(boos)*

And Judah was the father of Perez and Zerah *(huh)*

Whose mother was Tamar who played the prostitute *(boos)*

For the sake of justice *(cheers)*

And Perez was the father of Hezron *(huh)*

And Hezron the father of Ram *(huh)*

And Ram the father of Amminidab *(huh)*

The father of Nashon, a fine captain of Israel *(cheers)*

And Nashon the father of Salmon *(huh)*

And Salmon the father of Boaz by Rahab, the prostitute *(boos)*

Who saved God's people *(cheers)*

And Boaz the father of Obed by Ruth, the faithful foreigner *(cheers and applause)*

And Obed the father of Jesse, the father of David the King *(cheers)*

And David was the father of Solomon *(cheers)*

By the wife of Uriah whom he had set up to be killed *(boos)*

And Solomon was the father of Rehoboam who was faithful to God for much of his reign *(cheers)*

But abandoned God for five years *(boos)*

And Reheboam was the father of Abijah who has fourteen wives *(cheers and boos)*

And Abijah was the father of Asa who abandoned God at the end of his life and died of gangrene of the feet *(moan)*

And Asa was the father of Jehoshaphat, the father of Joram, the father of Uzziah whose pride brought his fall *(boos)*

And Uzziah was the father of Jotham, a very good king in every way *(cheers)*

And Jotham was the father of Ahaz, a very bad king in every way *(boos)*

And Ahaz was the father of Hezekiah who restored the kingdom to piety and justice *(cheers and applause)*

And Hezekiah was the father of Manasseh who ruled as king for fifty-five years *(cheers)*

And was evil for all fifty-five years *(boos)* (that is more than eleven re-elections!?)

And Manasseh was the father of Amos, the father of Josiah who was the father of Jechoniah and his brothers who were all faithful to God throughout their lives *(cheers and applause)*

And who were all deported to Babylon *(huh)*

And after the deportation to Babylon, Jechoniah was the father of Shealtiel *(huh)*

Who was the father of Zerubbabel, wise governor chosen by God *(cheers)*

And Zerubbabel was the father of Abiud *(huh)*

The father of Eliakim *(huh)*

Who was the father of Azor *(huh)*

Father of Zadok *(huh)*

Father of Achim *(huh)*

Who was the father of Eliud *(huh)*

Who was the father of Eleazar *(huh)*

The father of Matthan *(huh)*

Who was the father of Jacob, the father of Joseph *(cheers)*

The husband of Mary *(applause)*

Of whom was born Jesus who is called Christ *(cheers and applause)*.

Christians

The distinction between Christians and other men does not lie in country or language or customs…. They follow local customs in clothing, food, and in the rest of life; and yet they exhibit the wonderfully paradoxical nature of their own citizenship. They live in their own countries, but as if they were resident aliens. They share all things as citizens and yet endure all things as if they were an underclass. Every foreign country is their homeland and every homeland a foreign country. They marry like everyone else, and have children: but they do not abort their young. They keep a common table but not a common bed. They live in the world but not in a worldly way. They enjoy a full life on earth, but their citizenship is in heaven. They obey the appointed laws, but they surpass the laws in their own lifestyle. They love everyone — and are universally derided. They are unknown — and roundly criticised. They are put to death — and gain life. They are poor but make many rich. They lack all things and yet have all things in abundance. They are dishonoured and are glorified in their dishonour…. They are abused and they call down blessings in return. When they do good they are beaten up as ne'er-do-wells: when they are beaten up they rejoice as men who are given a new life…. In short, what the soul is in the body, the Christians are in the world. The soul lives in the body but is not confined by the body, and the Christians live in the world but are not confined by the world…. God has appointed them to this great calling, and it would be wrong for them to decline it.

Chapters five and six of an ancient book *The Epistle to Diognetus*, which was written in the second century.

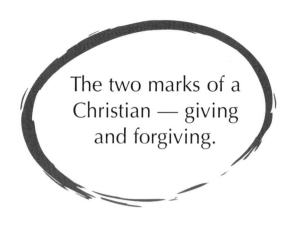

The two marks of a Christian — giving and forgiving.

Christians may not see eye to eye but they can walk arm in arm.

A true Christian is a person who is right side up in a world that is upside down.

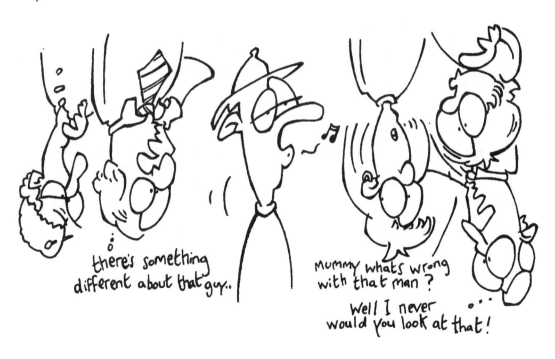

Church

It's a sobering thought that there are ten times more evangelicals in Brazil than in the whole of Europe put together. In 1570, Europe was 70% evangelical. Today it is nearer 7%.

In England, church membership has dropped 50% in the last 30 years. Only 10% of adults and 14% of children attend church. Since 1980, 7 churches a week have been closing. Over 300 young people left every week in the 90s.

In Denmark, 90% of the population have formal ties with the Lutheran Church but Sunday attendance in most parishes hovers around the 2.5% mark. The situation in Norway is similar.

In Sweden the situation is dire. 99% of the population professed Christianity in 1900, 64% do today. Of this 64% only 5% attend church. Half the population has no Christian faith at all.

In France the situation is desperate. 43 million people have no real link with any church. 98% of the French population is unreached. 1 in 20 French people own a Bible. 80% have never handled one.

The situation in Germany isn't much better. Only 5% of those who belong formally to the Protestant church are actively involved. There has been a mass exodus from the historic churches.

As the light of Christianity has decreased, so the darkness has increased. Even the name Europe signifies this. It derives from a Greek goddess raped by Zeus. Can't get more pagan than that!

In fact, paganism, occultism, and other religions have begun to increase in popularity during this century. There is a widespread interest in the New Age and the occult throughout Europe.

An estimated 90% of the population of Portugal consults spiritist mediums and witches. There are 100,000 full-time consulting magicians in Italy (three times the number of Catholic priests).

In Austria the number of active cult members outnumbers the Christians. In Iceland more than 40% of the population has been involved in the occult. In the UK, New Age religion is growing in popularity.

People are turning to other religions too. By 2004 there will be more Muslims than Anglicans in England. In a special January 1999 issue of *Time*, Islam was the only religion mentioned in the 'Spirit' section.

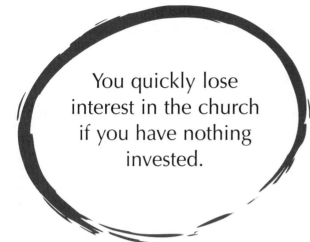

You quickly lose interest in the church if you have nothing invested.

The world at its worst needs the church at its best.

A cold church is like cold butter. It never spreads very well.

The church that does not evangelise will fossilise.

Coffee

You know you're addicted to coffee when

You're the employee of the month at the local coffee house and you don't even work there.

Your eyes stay open when you sneeze.

You chew on other people's fingernails.

You can type sixty words per minute with your feet.

You can jump-start your car without cables.

You don't sweat, you percolate.

You've worn out the handle on your favourite mug.

You walk twenty miles on your treadmill before you realise it's not hooked up.

You've worn the finish off your coffee table.

You're so wired, you pick up AM radio.

Your birthday is a national holiday in Brazil.

You'd be willing to spend time in a Turkish prison.

You go to sleep just so you can wake up and smell the coffee.

You're offended when people use the word 'brew' to mean beer.

You name your cats 'Cream' and 'Sugar'.

Your lips are permanently stuck in the sipping position.

You have a picture of your coffee mug on your coffee mug.

You don't tan, you roast.

You don't get mad, you get steamed.

Your coffee mug is insured by Lloyds of London.

You introduce your spouse as your coffee mate.

You think CPR stands for 'Coffee Provides Resuscitation'.

You ski uphill.

You get a speeding ticket even when you're parked.

You haven't blinked since the last lunar eclipse.

You just completed another sweater and you don't know how to knit.

Anon

Commandments

Above all else love God alone;
Bow down to neither wood nor stone.

God's name refuse to take in vain;
The Sabbath rest with care maintain.

Respect your parents all your days;
Hold sacred human life always.

Be loyal to your chosen mate;
Steal nothing, neither small nor great.

Report, with truth, your neighbour's deed;
And rid your mind of selfish greed.

Elton Trueblood

> Men and women are able creatures; we have made over 32 million laws and haven't yet improved on the Ten Commandments.

Commitment

Guidance means I can count on God. Commitment means God can count on me.

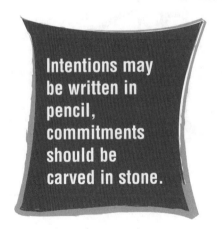

Intentions may be written in pencil, commitments should be carved in stone.

A prayer of John Wesley

I am no longer my own but yours,
Put me to what you will.
Put me to doing, put me to suffering.
Let me be employed for you, or laid
    aside for you.
Let me be full, let me be empty.
Let me have all things, let me have
    nothing.
I freely and wholeheartedly yield all
    things to
Your pleasure and disposal.
And now glorious and blessed God,
Father, Son and Holy Spirit,
You are mine and I am yours. So be it.
And this covenant now made on earth,
Let it be satisfied in heaven.

Amen.

A friend was in front of me coming out of church one day, and the preacher was standing at the door as he always is to shake hands. He grabbed my friend by the hand and pulled him aside. The pastor said to him, 'You need to join the army of the Lord!'

My friend replied, 'I'm already in the army of the Lord, pastor.'

The pastor questioned, 'How come I don't see you except at Christmas and Easter?'

He whispered back, 'I'm in the secret service.'

Three vicars were having lunch together. One said, 'You know, since summer started I've been having trouble with bats at church. I've tried everything — noise, spray, cats — nothing seems to scare them away.'

Another said, 'Yes, me too. I've got hundreds living in my belfry. I've even had the place fumigated, and they still won't go away.'

The third said, 'I baptised all mine, and made them members of the church…. Haven't seen one back since!'

Eight things you never hear in church

1. It's my turn to sit in the front pew.
2. I was so enthralled, I never noticed your sermon went twenty-five minutes over time.
3. Personally I find witnessing much more enjoyable than golf.
4. I volunteer to be a permanent teacher for the Sunday school.
5. Forget the denominational minimum salary, let's pay our pastor so he can live like we do.
6. I love it when we sing hymns I've never heard before.
7. Pastor, we'd like to send you to this conference in the Bahamas.
8. Nothing inspires me and strengthens my commitment like our annual stewardship campaign.

❝ I'd rather stand trial before people for serving
God than to stand trial before God for serving people. ❞

A commitment is
doing what you said
you would do, long
after the feeling you
said it in has passed.

'If a person
doesn't have
something to
die for, they are
not fit to live.'
Martin Luther
King, Jr.

Communication

What do you mean we don't communicate? Just
yesterday I faxed you a reply to the recorded message
you left on my answerphone.

Old Fred had been a faithful Christian and was in the hospital, near death. The family called their preacher to stand with them. As the preacher stood next to the bed, Fred's condition appeared to deteriorate and he motioned frantically for something to write on. The pastor lovingly handed him a pen and a piece of paper, and Fred used his last bit of energy to scribble a note, then suddenly died.

The preacher thought it best not to look at the note at that time, so he placed it in his jacket pocket. At the funeral, as he was finishing the message, he realised that he was wearing the same jacket that he was wearing when Fred died.

He said, 'You know, Fred handed me a note just before he died. I haven't looked at it, but knowing Fred, I'm sure there's a word of inspiration there for us all.'

He opened the note, and read, 'Please step to your left — you're standing on my oxygen tube!'

A little girl was in church with her mother when she started feeling ill.

'Mummy,' she said, 'can we leave now?'

'No,' her mother replied.

'Well, I think I'm going to throw up!'

'Then go out the front door and around to the back of the church and throw up behind a bush.'

After about sixty seconds the little girl returned to her seat.

'Did you throw up?' Mum asked.

'Yes.'

'How could you have gone all the way to the back of the church and returned so quickly?'

'I didn't have to go out of the church, Mummy. They have a box next to the front door that says, "For the sick".'

An English lady is buying a house in Switzerland. On returning home she realises that she didn't see the toilet in her new house. She therefore writes to the estate agent asking the whereabouts of the WC. The estate agent has very little knowledge of the English language and so asks the parish priest to translate the letter to him. The only equivalent of WC that he can think of is the wayside chapel. This reply is therefore received by the English lady.

My Dear Madam,

I take great pleasure in informing you that the WC is situated nine miles from the house in the centre of a beautiful grove of pine trees surrounded by lovely grounds.

It is capable of holding 229 people, and it is open on Sundays and Thursdays only. As there are a great number of people expected during the summer months, I suggest that you come early, although there is usually standing room. This is an unfortunate situation, especially if you are in the habit of going regularly. It may interest you to know that my daughter was married in the WC and it was there that she met her husband. I can remember the rush for seats. There were ten people to every seat usually occupied by one. It was wonderful to see the expressions on their faces.

You will be glad to hear that a good number of people bring their lunch and make a day of it, while those who can afford to go by car arrive just in time. I would especially recommend your Ladyship to go on Thursdays where there is an organ accompaniment. The acoustics are excellent, even the most delicate sounds can be heard everywhere.

The newest addition is a bell donated by a wealthy resident of the district. It rings every time a person enters. A bazaar is to be held to provide plush seats for all, since the people feel it is long needed. My wife is rather delicate and she cannot attend regularly. It is almost a year since she went last, and naturally it pains her very much not to be able to go more often.

I shall be delighted to reserve the best seat for you, where you shall be seen by all. For the children there is a special day and time so that they do not disturb the elders. Hoping to be of some service to you.

Yours faithfully,

Confession

A man with a nagging secret couldn't keep it any longer. In the confessional he admitted that for years he had been stealing building supplies from the lumberyard where he worked.

'What did you take?' his priest asked.

'Enough to build my own house and enough for my son's house. And houses for our two daughters and our cottage at the lake.'

'This is very serious,' the priest said. 'I shall have to think of a far-reaching penance. Have you ever done a retreat?'

'No, Father, I haven't,' the man replied. 'But if you can get the plans, I can get the lumber.'

It is better for people to confess their sins than to harden their hearts.

Consumerism

'Religion tends to be strongest when life is hard... a person whose main difficulty is not crop failure but video breakdown has less need of the consolations and promises of religion.'

Robert Bork

(Hymns: the way we'd sing them if we were honest)

I Surrender, Some
Fill My Spoon, Lord
He's Quite a Bit to Me
Take My Life and Let Me Be
When the Saints Go Sneaking in
Sit Up, Sit Up for Jesus
A Comfy Mattress Is Our God
Self-esteem to the World, the Lord Is Come
Oh, for a Couple of Tongues to Sing
Praise God from whom all Affirmations Flow
My Hope Is Built on Nothing Much
Pillow of Ages, Fluffed for Me
I'm Fairly Certain that My Redeemer Lives
What an Acquaintance We Have in Jesus
Above Average Is thy Faithfulness
We Are Milling Around in the Light of God
Spirit of the Living God, Fall Somewhere Near Me

Convictions

A belief is something you hold. A conviction is something that holds you.

People generally have too many opinions and not enough convictions.

Cosmetics

Michelle Pfeiffer appeared on the cover of a magazine with the caption 'What Michelle Pfeiffer needs is… absolutely nothing'. It was later discovered by a reporter that Michelle Pfeiffer did need something after all, she needed $1,525 of touch-up work on that cover photo. From the touch-up artist's bill there is a partial list of things that were done to make Michelle Pfeiffer look beautiful:

Clean up complexion
Soften eye lines
Soften smile line
Add colour to lips
Trim chin
Remove neck lines
Soften line under ear lobe
Add highlights to earrings
Add blush to cheek
Clean up neck line
Remove stray hair
Remove hair strand on dress
Adjust colour and add hair on top of head
Add dress on side to create better line
Add forehead
Add dress on shoulder
Soften neck muscle a bit
Clean up and smooth dress folds under arm
    and create one seam on image on right side

Total price: $1,525

Cost

When someone (especially a doctor or a dentist) says to you, 'We're only doing this for your own good,' you immediately know two things:

1. It's going to hurt like mad.
2. It's going to cost a fortune.

Criticism

The difference between coaching and criticism is your attitude.

I can complain because rose bushes have thorns or rejoice because the thorn bush has a rose. It's all up to me.

Don't criticise too quickly. Even a clock that doesn't work is right twice a day.

Ten people talked three million Israelites out of entering the Promised Land — that's how dangerous a vocal minority can be.

I owed a debt which I couldn't pay.
Christ paid a debt that he didn't owe.

 Morality will keep you out of jail, but only the blood of Jesus will keep you out of hell.

It's the picture of violence
Yet the key to peace

A picture of suffering
Yet the key to healing

A picture of death
Yet the key to life

A picture of utter weakness
Yet the key to power

A picture of capital punishment
Yet the key to mercy and
      forgiveness

A picture of vicious hatred
Yet the key to love

A picture of supreme shame
Yet the Christian's supreme boast.

David Watson

Culture

Alice Bailey has played a big part in influencing Western minds. She was born in 1880. She made a pact with a demonic Grand Master and opened her spirit to guides from the spirit world, including a master from the Tibetan world. She wrote many books, claiming she was dictating what the spirit guide said. Her main book is called *The Plan*. What is the plan? To set people free from the restrictions of Christianity so that they can enjoy the liberty of life. The principles of this book have been implemented in the Western world as law. Here are the ten strategies of 'The Plan'

1. Push God out of the schools. If the people grow up without reference to God, then they will consider God irrelevant to day-to-day life.

2. Break the traditional Judaeo-Christian Family Concept. Break communication between parents and children so that parents can't pass on spiritual values to their children. Do this by pushing excessive child rights.

3. Remove the restrictions on sex. Sex is the biggest joy and Christianity robs people of this. People must be freed to enjoy it without restrictions. It's not just for marrieds, it's for everybody.

4. Since sex is the greatest expression of man's enjoyment of life, man must be free to express sex in ALL its forms. Homosexuality, orgies, even bestiality are desirable so long as no one is being abused or harmed.

5. People must be free to abort unwanted children. If a man can have sex and then live without the consequences then the same should be true for a woman too. A woman must have the right to abort an unwanted child.

6. Every person develops soul bonds, so when a soul bond wears out a person must be free to divorce. When a new one starts to grow, one must be free to get together with that person even if they are married.

7. Defuse religious radicalism. Christianity says Jesus is the only way. Defuse this by: a) silencing Christianity; and b) promoting other faiths (the creation of inter-faith harmony).

8. Use the media to influence mass opinion. Create mass opinion that is receptive to these values by using TV, film, the press, etc. (NB: In the African church, what Western believers call normal would be pornography.)

9. Debase art in all its forms. Corrupt music, painting, poetry and every expression of the heart and make it obscene, immoral and occultic. Debase the arts in every way possible.

10. Get the church to endorse every one of these nine strategies. Get the churches to accept these principles and to say they're OK (then legal ground is given for these values to get a foothold).

(Paraphrase by Mark Stibbe of John Mulinde's account of Alice Bailey's writings, presented at the Europe Awake Conference at St Andrew's, Chorleywood, in October 1999.)

D

Death

> Now I lay me down to sleep
> I pray thee, Lord, my soul to keep;
> And if I die before I wake,
> I pray that Jesus ain't a fake.

A new business was opening and one of the owner's friends wanted to send him flowers for the occasion. They arrived at the new business site and the owner read the card, 'Rest in Peace'.

The owner was angry and called the florist to complain. After he had told the florist of the obvious mistake and how angry he was, the florist replied, 'Sir, I'm really sorry for the mistake, but rather than getting angry you should imagine this.

'Somewhere there is a funeral taking place today, and they have flowers with a note saying, "Congratulations on your new location!"'

Chamber's coffins are just fine;
Made of sandalwood and pine.
If your loved ones have to go
Call Columbus 6-9-0.
If your loved ones pass away
Have them pass the Chamber's way.
Chamber's customers all sing
'Death, O Death, where is thy sting?'

Consider the case of the Illinois man who left the snow-filled streets of Chicago for a vacation in Florida. His wife was on a business trip and was planning to meet him there the next day. When he reached his hotel, he decided to send his wife a quick e-mail. Unable to find the scrap of paper on which he had written her e-mail address, he did his best to type it in from memory. Unfortunately, he missed one letter, and his note was directed instead to a preacher's wife, whose husband had passed away only the day before.

When the grieving widow checked her e-mail, she took one look at the monitor and let out a piercing scream, and fell to the floor in a dead faint. At the sound, her family rushed into the room and saw this note on the screen:

Dearest Wife,

Just got checked in. Everything prepared for your arrival tomorrow.

PS. Sure is hot down here.

The old American preacher was dying at home in his bed. He realised his time was short, so he sent for his doctor and his lawyer to come to his home. When they arrived, they were shown up to his bedroom. As they entered the room, the preacher held out his hands and motioned for them to sit on each side of the bed. For a very long time, no one said a word. Finally, the doctor spoke up and said, 'Preacher, you're not long for this world, you'd better tell us why you asked us to come.' The preacher mustered up all his strength and in a strained voice said, 'Well, Jesus died between two thieves and that's how I wanted to die.'

A sister and brother are talking to each other when the little boy gets up and walks over to his grandpa and says, 'Grandpa, please make a frog noise.'

The grandpa says, 'No.'

The little boy goes on, 'Please… please make a frog noise.'

The grandpa says, 'No, now go and play.'

The little boy then says to his sister, 'Go and tell Grandpa to make a frog noise.' So the little girl goes to her grandpa and says, 'Please make a frog noise.'

The grandpa says, 'I just told your brother no and I'm telling you no.'

The little girl says, 'Please… please Grandpa make a frog noise.'

The grandpa says, 'Why do you want me to make a frog noise?'

The little girl replies, 'Because Mummy said when you croak we can go to Disney world!'

There was a woman who had been diagnosed with a terminal illness and had been given three months to live. So as she was getting her things in order, she contacted her pastor and had him come to her house to discuss certain aspects of her final wishes.

She told him which songs she wanted sung at the service, what scriptures she would like read, and what outfit she wanted to be buried in. The woman also requested to be buried with her favourite Bible. Everything was in order and the pastor was preparing to leave when the woman suddenly remembered something very important to her.

'There's one more thing,' she said excitedly.

'What's that?' came the pastor's reply.

'This is very important,' the woman continued. 'I want to be buried with a fork in my right hand.'

The pastor stood looking at the woman, not knowing quite what to say.

'That surprises you, doesn't it?' the woman asked.

'Well, to be honest, I'm puzzled by the request,' said the pastor.

The woman explained. 'In all my years of attending church socials and suppers, I always remember that when the dishes of the main course were being cleared, someone would inevitably lean over and say, "Keep your fork." It was my favourite part because I knew that something better was coming... like velvety chocolate cake or apple pie and cream. Something wonderful, and with substance!

'So, I just want people to see me there in that coffin with a fork in my hand. And I want them to wonder "What's with the fork?" Then I want you to tell them: "Keep your fork... the best is yet to come."'

The American Way of Death

Not	But
The body	the remains
The corpse	Mr Jones
Morgue	preparation room
Coffin	casket of rest
Undertaker	mortician
Laying-out room	slumber room
Dead	deceased, passed away
Hearse	casket couch
Death certificate	vital statistics form
Graveyard	memorial
Cost of the funeral	amount of investment in the service

Denial

'I have never done anything bad to anyone. Never. And that is one of the things that I am proud of — I have never hurt anybody. I have never been vicious about anybody, never taken any drugs, never tricked anyone; on the contrary, I can say that many many people have done it to me — men, husbands, business associates, lawyers, the list is endless…I basically think that when one meets one's maker, if I do, there won't be anything I've done that I need to be ashamed of. Nothing.'

Actress Joan Collins, interviewed in *The Sunday Telegraph*

Determination

Curious people ask questions. Determined people find answers.

Some people succeed because they are destined to, but most people succeed because they are determined to.

A dead fish can float downstream but it takes a living fish to swim upstream.

Diligence

What we hope to do with ease we must first learn to do with diligence.

Doctrine

'If a man has only correct doctrine to offer me, I am sure to slip out at the first intermission to seek the company of someone who has seen for himself how lovely is the face of him who is the rose of Sharon and the lily of the valley. Such a man can help me, and no one else can.'

A. W. Tozer

Doublespeak

> Meaningful downturn in aggregate output (recession)
> After-sales service (kickback)
> Resource development park (rubbish dump)
> Temporarily displaced inventory (stolen goods)
> Strategic misrepresentation (lie)
> Reality augmentation (lie)
> Terminological inexactitude (lie)
>
> **William Lutz**

Dying

Srinivasa Ramanujan, the Indian mathematical genius, is called a phenomenal genius by the *Encyclopaedia Britannica*. He was very poor, but somehow picked up a couple of books of mathematical theorems (six thousand of them!), mastered them and then produced a few of his own.

He received a scholarship to Madras University, but was thrown out because he refused to study anything but mathematics: he failed all his other courses. He ended up at Cambridge University, became a Fellow of the Royal Society and a friend of the great mathematician Hardy.

Then came disaster. Ramanujan contracted tuberculosis. When he was extremely sick, and in fact dying, Hardy ordered a taxi in order to take him to hospital. As they got out of the taxi Hardy, aware of the seriousness of the occasion, commented that it seemed vaguely absurd to be making a vital journey in a prosaic London taxi, with the insignificant number 1729. Ramanujan responded weakly, 'No, Hardy, no, you are wrong. It is the lowest number expressible as the sum of two cubes in two different ways!' and then he died.

First thought: Was Ramanujan right? He was. One cubed plus twelve cubed or nine cubed plus ten cubed gives 1729. And it can't be done for any smaller number. Second thought: What a strange thing for a genius on the edge of eternity to be thinking about.

Endurance

'Great faith is a product of great fights. Great testimonies are the outcome of great tests. Great triumphs can only come after great trials.'

Smith Wigglesworth

Ten little Christians standing in a line,
One disliked the preacher, then there were nine.
Nine little Christians stayed up very late,
One overslept on Sunday and then there were eight.
Eight little Christians on their way to heaven,
One took the low road and then there were seven.
Seven little Christians chirping like chicks,
One disliked the music, then there were six.
Six little Christians very much alive,
But one lost their interest and then there were five.
Five little Christians pulling for heaven's shore,
But one stopped to take a rest, and then there were four.
Four little Christians each busy as a bee,
One got their feelings hurt, and then there were three.
Three little Christians knew not what to do,
One joined the sports club, and then there were two.
Two little Christians, our rhyme is nearly done,
Differed with each other, then there was none!

Anon

The following was taken from registration sheets and comment cards returned to the staff of the Bridger Wilderness Area in Wyoming in 1996:

1. Trails need to be wider so people can walk holding hands.
2. Trails need to be reconstructed. Please avoid building trails that go uphill.
3. Too many bugs and leeches and spiders and spiders' webs. Please spray the wilderness to rid the area of these pests.
4. Please pave the trails so they can be ploughed clear of snow during the winter.
5. Chairlifts need to be in some places so that we can get to wonderful views without having to hike to them.
6. The coyotes made too much noise last night and kept me awake. Please eradicate these annoying animals.
7. A small deer came into my camp and stole my jar of pickles. Is there a way I can get reimbursed?
8. Reflectors need to be placed on trees every fifty feet so people can hike at night with flashlights.
9. Escalators would help on steep uphill sections.
10. A McDonald's would be nice at the trailhead.
11. The places where trails do not exist are not well marked.
12. Too many rocks in the mountains.

Epitaphs

On the grave of Ezekial Aikle in East Dalhousie Cemetery, Nova Scotia:

Here lies
Ezekial Aikle
Age 102
The good
Die young.

In a cemetery in Ribbesford.

*The children of Israel wanted bread
And the Lord sent them manna,
Old clerk Wallace wanted a wife,
And the devil sent him Anna.*

Memory of an accident in a cemetery in Uniontown, Pennsylvania:

Here lies the body
of Jonathan Blake
Stepped on the gas
Instead of the brake.

A lawyer's (Sir John Strange) epitaph in England:

**Here lies an honest lawyer,
And that is Strange.**

In a cemetery in London.

**Here lies Ann Mann,
Who lived an old maid
But died an old Mann.
8th December 1767**

Playing with names in a cemetery in Ruidoso, New Mexico:

Here lies
Johnny Yeast
Pardon me
For not rising.

In a cemetery in Silver City, Nevada:

Here lays Butch,
We planted him raw.
He was quick on the trigger,
But slow on the draw.

John Penny's epitaph in the cemetery in Wimborne:

*Reader if cash thou art
In want of any
Dig four feet deep
And thou wilt find a Penny.*

In a cemetery in Hartscombe:

**On the 22nd of June
— Jonathan Fiddle —
Went out of tune.**

Harry Edsel Smith of Albany, New York:

Born 1903 — Died 1942
Looked up the elevator shaft to see if the car was on the way down. It was.

Escapism

'Men occasionally stumble over the truth, but most pick themselves up and hurry off as if nothing had happened.'
Winston Churchill

Eternity

Those who live as if there was no after-life will gain nothing if they are proved to be right and will lose everything if they are proved to be wrong. Those who live as if the present influences the next world, have lost nothing if they are proved to be wrong and will have gained everything if they are proved to be right.

Blaise Pascal: Born 19 June 1923 – Died 19 August 1962

Evangelism

God doesn't command sinners to go to church, but he does command the church to go to sinners.

An Islamic commentator said this about the influence of Franciscan monks in the Middle East.

The only missionaries we fear are the Franciscan monks. For 700 years they have given us fits. Our approach is to persuade potential converts with apologetics. We're great at arguing, but that doesn't work with the Franciscans. Instead of engaging us, they quietly go about our cities, serving everyone. Once people are served they become interested in Christianity, and the next thing you know they've become followers of Jesus. Those Franciscan Christians don't fight fair with us!

'It has been estimated that in spite of the combined efforts of all the churches and missionary agencies put together, it is taking 1,000 Christians an average of 365 days to win one person to Christ. This is not good enough.'

Dr Leighton Ford

'Jesus was born in a borrowed manger. He preached from a borrowed boat. He entered Jerusalem on a borrowed donkey, he ate the Last Supper in a borrowed upper room and he was buried in a borrowed tomb. Now he asks to borrow the lives of Christians to reach the rest of the world. If we do not speak, then he is dumb and silent.'

Dr Leighton Ford

A missionary called John Vassar knocked on the door of a person's home and asked the lady if she knew Christ. She said, 'It's none of your business!' and slammed the door in his face. He stood on the doorstep and wept and wept. She was looking out of her window at him weeping. The next Sunday she presented herself for church membership. She said it was those tears.

Now it came to pass that a group existed who called themselves fishermen. There were many fish in the waters all around. Week after week, month after month, and year after year, the fishermen met in meetings and talked about their call to fish, the abundance of fish and how they might go about fishing.

Year after year, they carefully defined what fishing means, defended fishing as an occupation, declared that fishing is always to be a primary task of fishermen, in fact, that there should be a Decade of Fishing!

Continually they searched for new and better methods of fishing. Further they said, 'The fishing industry exists by fishing as fire exists by burning.' They loved slogans such as 'Fishing is the task of every fisherman', and 'Every Fisherman is a fisher'. They sponsored costly nationwide and worldwide congresses to discuss fishing issues such as the new fishing equipment, fish calls, and whether any new bait had been discovered.

Many who felt the call to be fishermen responded. They were commissioned and sent to fish. They engaged in all kinds of occupations. They built power plants to pump water for fish and tractors to plough new waterways. They made all kinds of equipment to travel here and there to look at fish hatcheries. Some also said that they wanted to be part of the fishing party, but they felt called to furnish fishing equipment. Others felt their job was to relate to the fish in a good way so the fish would know the difference between good and bad fishermen. Others felt that simply letting the fish know they were nice, land-loving neighbours and how loving and kind they were was enough.

These fishermen built large beautiful buildings called 'Fishing Headquarters'. The plea was that everyone should be a fisherman and every fisherman should fish. One thing they didn't do, however – they didn't fish.

After one stirring meeting on 'The necessity of fishing', one young man left the meeting and went fishing. The next day he reported that he had caught two fish. He was honoured for his excellent catch and scheduled to visit all the big meetings possible to tell how he did it. So he left his fishing in order to have time to tell other fishermen about the experience. He was also placed on the Fishermen's General Board as a person having considerable experience.

Now it's true that many of the fishermen sacrificed and put up with all kinds of difficulties. Some lived near the water and bore the smell of dead fish every day. They received the ridicule of some who made fun of their fishermens' clubs and the fact that they claimed to be fishermen yet never fished. They wondered about those who felt it was of little use to attend the weekly meetings to talk about fishing. After all, were they not following the Master who said, 'Follow me and I will make you fishers of men'?

John Wesley told his co-workers:

> You have nothing to do but save souls. Therefore spend and be spent in this work. It is not your business to preach so many times and to take care of this or that society, but to save as many souls as you can, to bring as many sinners as you possibly can to repentance and with all your power to build them up in that holiness without which they cannot see the Lord.

Excuses

The following is a series of quotes taken from insurance or accident forms. They are the actual words of people who tried to summarise their encounters with trouble.

- **Coming home, I drove into the wrong house and collided with a tree I don't have.**
- The other car collided with mine without giving warning of its intentions.
- *I thought my window was down, but I found it was up when I put my hand through it.*
- I collided with a stationary vehicle coming the other way.
- ***A van backed through my windscreen into my wife's face.***
- A pedestrian hit me and went under my car.
- *The guy was all over the road; I had to swerve a number of times before I hit him.*
- I pulled away from the side of the road, glanced at my mother-in-law, and headed over the embankment.
- **In my attempt to kill a fly, I drove into a telephone pole.**
- I had been shopping for plants all day and was on my way home. As I reached an intersection, a hedge sprang up obscuring my vision. I did not see the other car.
- *I had been driving for forty years when I fell asleep at the wheel and had an accident.*
- **I was on the way to the doctor's with rear-end trouble when my universal joint gave way, causing me to have an accident.**
- To avoid hitting the bumper of the car in front, I struck the pedestrian.
- *As I approached the intersection, a stop sign suddenly appeared in a place where no stop sign had ever appeared before. I was unable to stop in time to avoid the accident.*
- My car was legally parked as it backed into the other vehicle.
- *An invisible car came out of nowhere, struck my vehicle, and vanished.*
- I told the police that I was not injured, but removing my hat, I found I had skull fracture.
- **The pedestrian had no idea which direction to go, so I ran over him.**
- *I was thrown from my car as it left the road. I was later found in a ditch by some stray cows.*
- The telephone pole was approaching fast. I attempted to swerve out of its path when it struck my front end.
- ***I was unable to stop in time and my car crashed into the other vehicle. The driver and passenger then left immediately for a holiday with injuries.***

The following are actual excuses for missing school that were handed in by pupils:

My son is under a doctor's care and could not take PE yesterday. Please execute him.

Please excuse Cynthia from being absent. He was sick and I had her shot.

Please excuse Tom for being absent on January 28, 29, 30, 31, 32 and 33.

Please excuse Danny for being, it was his father's fault.

Julie could not come to school yesterday because she was bothered by very close veins.

Richard had an acre in his side.

Please excuse Tom for being absent last week, he could not talk because of Larry and Gitus.

Please excuse Nancy for staying home. The doctor said that her lungs are too full to be outside.

Please excuse Robert from being absent, he had a cold and could not breed well.

Facts

'Facts do not cease to exist because they are ignored.'
Aldous Huxley

A good way to stop a red-hot argument is to lay a few cold facts on it.

Digging for facts is better than jumping to conclusions.

Failure

'Only those who dare to fail greatly can ever achieve greatly.'
Robert F Kennedy

Failure should be our teacher, not our undertaker.

Failure is a temporary detour, not a dead-end street.

 Failure is delay, not defeat.

Faith

Faith hears the inaudible, sees the invisible, believes the incredible and receives the impossible.

People who have no faith in themselves seldom have faith in others.

If doubts overtake you, stop for a faith lift.

'To me, faith is not just a noun but a verb.'
Jimmy Carter, former President of the United States

When Michael Faraday, the great English physicist, was dying, friends gathered at his bedside. As was often the case in the nineteenth century, they sought some final words from the dying man. 'What are your speculations?' they asked.

His answer was firm. 'Speculations! I have none. I am resting on certainties.'

Positive thinking without positive faith will result in positive failure.

It is impossible for faith to overdraw its account in the bank of heaven.

Faithfulness

A man goes into a photography shop with a framed picture of his girlfriend. He wanted another copy of the photo. This involved removing it from the frame. The assistant noticed the inscription on the back of the photograph.

'Me dearest Tom, I love you with all my heart. I love you more and more each day. I will love you for ever and ever. I am yours for all eternity.' Signed Diane.

And it contained a PS: 'If we ever break up, I want this picture back.'

Fear

'He who fears he shall suffer, already suffers what he fears.' **Montaigne**

Courage is fear that has said its prayers.

Don't fear tomorrow. God is already there.

'All adventures, especially into new territory, are scary.' **Sally Ride, Astronaut**

'Fear is the darkroom where Satan develops your negatives.' **Francis Frangipane**

Feelings

'Feelings come and feelings go and feelings are deceiving. My warrant is the word of God, naught else is worth believing.' **Martin Luther King, Jr**

Flying

Here are some statements actually made by airline attendants who were trying to make their 'in-flight safety talk' more interesting:

'There may be fifty ways to leave your lover, but there are only four ways out of this aeroplane'.

'Smoking in the lavatories is prohibited. Anyone caught smoking in the lavatories will be asked to leave the plane immediately.'

'We are pleased to have some of the best flight attendants in the industry. Unfortunately none of them is on this flight.'

After a particularly bumpy landing, one elderly lady looked the captain in the eye and said, 'Did we land or were we shot down?'

'Welcome aboard flight XYZ. To operate your seatbelt, insert the metal tab into the buckle, and pull tight. It works just like every other seatbelt, and if you don't know how to operate one, you probably shouldn't be out in public unsupervised. In the event of a sudden loss of cabin pressure, oxygen masks will descend from the ceiling. Stop screaming, grab the mask and pull it over your face. If you have a small child travelling with you, secure your mask before assisting theirs. If you are travelling with two small children, decide now which one you love more.'

'Thank you for flying XYZ Airlines. We hope you enjoyed giving us the business as much as we enjoyed taking you for a ride.'

'Your seat cushions can be used for flotation, and in the event of an emergency water landing, please take them with our compliments.'

Another flight attendant's comment on a less-than-perfect landing: 'We ask you to please remain seated as Captain Kangaroo bounces us to the terminal.'

Once on a Southwest Airlines flight, the pilot said, 'We've reached our cruising altitude now, and I'm turning off the seat belt sign. I'm switching to auto pilot, too, so I can come back there and visit with all of you for the rest of the flight.'

As the plane landed and was coming to a stop at Washington National Airport, a lone voice comes over the loudspeaker: 'Whoa, big feller... WHOA!'

'Should the cabin lose pressure, oxygen masks will drop from the overhead area. Please place the bag over your own mouth and nose before assisting children or adults acting like children.'

'As you exit the plane, please make sure you gather all of your belongings. Anything left behind will be distributed evenly among the flight attendants. Please do not leave children or spouses.'

'Last one off the plane must clean it.'

'We do feature a smoking section on this flight; if you must smoke, contact a member of the flight crew and we will escort you to the wing of the aeroplane.'

'Weather at our destination is 50 degrees with some broken clouds, but they'll try to have them fixed before we arrive. Thank you, and remember, nobody loves you, or your money, more than Southwest Airlines.'

Forgiveness

'The weak can never forgive. Forgiveness is the attribute of the strong.' **Mahatma Gandhi**

'Jesus came to rub it out not rub it in.' **J. John**

People with clenched fists cannot shake hands.

Friendship

'If you live to be a hundred, I want to live to be a hundred minus one day, so I never have to live without you.' **Winnie the Pooh**

'True friendship is like sound health; the value of it is seldom known until it is lost.' **Charles Colton**

'A real friend is one who walks in when the rest of the world walks out.'

'Don't walk in front of me, I may not follow. Don't walk behind me, I may not lead. Walk beside me and be my friend.' **Albert Camus**

'Friendship is one mind in two bodies.' **Mencius**

'Hold a true friend with both your hands.' **Nigerian proverb**

The best vitamin for making friends is... B1.

G

Gentiles

A man returns home from the doctor and tells his wife:

'Edith, the doctor says I have herpes.'

'What's that?' she says, as she reaches out for the dictionary. She then lets out a sigh of relief and says, 'There is nothing to worry about, it says right here (pointing at the dictionary), it is a disease of the gentiles.'

Giving

Three boys are in the playground bragging about their fathers. The first boy says, 'My dad scribbles a few words on a piece of paper, he calls it a poem, they give him £50.'

The second boy says, 'That's nothing. My dad scribbles a few words on a piece of paper, he calls it a song, they give him £100.'

The third boy says, 'I've beaten you both. My dad scribbles a few words on a piece of paper, he calls it a sermon. And it takes eight people to collect all the money!'

A 50p piece met a £5 note and said, 'Hey! Where have you been? I haven't seen you around here much.'

The £5 note replied, 'I've been hanging out at the Bingo, done the Lottery a few times, had a Chinese takeaway, gone to a couple of football matches, a bit of shopping, holidays abroad, that kind of stuff. How about you?'

The 50p piece sighed and said, 'Oh, you know. Same old stuff — church, church, church.'

The principal hindrance to the advancement of the kingdom of God is greed. It is the chief obstacle to heaven sent revival. It seems that when the back of greed is broken, your human spirit soars in regions of unselfishness. I believe it is safe to say there can be no continuous revival without 'hilarious' giving. And I fear no contradiction: wherever there is 'hilarious' giving there will be continuous revival.

O.S Hawkins

'[My wife and I] measure the success of the year on how much we give away. The bulk of it goes to church and related activities.'
Novelist John Grisham in *USA Today* (2/11/99)

'I'm afraid biblical charity is more than merely giving away that which we could afford to do without anyway.'

C S Lewis

After church one Sunday morning, a mother commented, 'The choir was awful this morning.'

The father commented, 'The sermon was too long.'

Their seven-year-old daughter added, 'But you've got to admit it was a pretty good show for 10p.'

Two men were shipwrecked on a desert island. The minute they got on to the island one of them started screaming and yelling, 'We're going to die! We're going to die! There's no food! No water! We're going to die!'

The second man was propped up against a palm tree and acting so calmly it drove the first man crazy. 'Don't you understand? We're going to die!'

The second man replied, 'You don't understand, I make £100,000 a week.'

The first man looked at him quite dumbfounded and asked, 'What difference does that make? We're on an island with no food and no water! We're going to DIE!'

The second man answered, 'You just don't get it. I make £100,000 a week and I tithe ten percent on that £100,000 a week. My pastor will find me!'

God

Written by Danny Dutton, age eight, from Chula Vista, California, for his third-grade homework assignment to 'Explain God'.

One of God's main jobs is making people. He makes them to replace the ones that die so there will be enough people to take care of things on earth. He doesn't make grown-ups, just babies. I think because they are smaller and easier to make. That way, he doesn't have to take up his valuable time teaching them to talk and walk. He can just leave that to mothers and fathers.

God's second most important job is listening to prayers. An awful lot of this goes on, since some people, like preachers and things, pray at times besides bed time. God doesn't have time to listen to the radio or TV because of this. Because he hears everything there must be a terrible lot of noise in His ears, unless he has thought of a way to turn it off. God sees everything and hears everything and is everywhere which keeps him pretty busy. So you shouldn't go wasting his time by going over your mum and dad's head asking for something they've said you can't have.

Atheists are people who don't believe in God. I don't think there are any in Chula Vista. At least there aren't any who come to our church.

Jesus is God's Son. He used to do all the hard work like walking on water and performing miracles and trying to teach the people who didn't want to learn about God. They finally got tired of him preaching to them and Jesus said they didn't know what they were doing and to forgive them and God said OK. His dad (God) appreciated everything that he had done and all his hard work on earth so he told him he didn't have to go out on the road any more, he could stay in heaven. So he did. And now he helps his dad out by listening to prayers and seeing things which are important for God to take care of and which ones he can take care of himself without having to bother God. Like a secretary only more important.

You can pray any time you want and they are sure to hear you because they got it worked out so one of them is on duty all the time. You should always go to church on Sunday because it makes God happy, and if there's anybody you want to make happy, it's God. Don't skip church to do something you think will be more fun like going to the beach. This is wrong! And, besides, the sun doesn't come out at the beach until noon anyway. If you don't believe in God, besides being an atheist, you will be very lonely, because your parents can't go everywhere with you, like to camp, but God can. It is good to know he's around you when you're scared in the dark or when you can't swim very good and you get thrown into real deep water by big kids.

But you shouldn't just always think of what God can do for you. I figure God put me here and he can take me back anytime he pleases. And that's why I believe in God.

Three engineers, a mechanical engineer, an electrical engineer and a civil engineer, are arguing about the nature of God. The mechanical engineer says, 'God must be a mechanical engineer. Look at the human body and what a marvel of mechanical engineering it is. The way the bones, muscles, tendons and ligaments all work together shows that God is a mechanical engineer.'

The electrical engineer says, 'No, you're wrong. God must be an electrical engineer. Look at the nerves, spinal cord and brain, and how they control the bones and muscles, and you will be convinced that God is an electrical engineer.'

The civil engineer says, 'You're both wrong. God *must* be a civil engineer, because who else but a civil engineer would consider putting a waste disposal pipeline through a recreational area.'

What a remarkable organ God has created in the human ear! In comparison with it, the most sophisticated computer (it has been said) is 'as crude as a concrete mixer'.

Of course what we usually call the ear is only the outer ear, that fleshy excrescence on the side of the head which comes in a variety of shapes and sizes. From it a one-inch canal leads to the ear drum, behind which is the middle ear, where the body's three tiniest bones (popularly known as the anvil, the hammer and the stirrup) amplify sound twenty-two times and pass it on to the inner ear, where the real hearing takes place. Its main component is the snail-shaped tube named the cochlea. It contains thousands of microscopic, hairlike cells, each of which is tuned to one particular vibration.

The vibrations are now converted into electric impulses which convey sound to the brain for decoding along 30,000 circuits of the auditory nerve, enough for a sizeable city's telephone service. The human ear has rightly been celebrated as 'a triumph of miniaturisation'.

'Prince Charles has many titles. He is the Heir Apparent to the Crown, His Royal Highness, the Prince of Wales, Duke of Cornwall, Knight of the Garter, Colonel in Chief of the Royal Regiment of Wales, Duke of Rothesay, Knight of the Thistle, Commander of the Royal Navy, Great Master of the Order of Bath, Earl of Chester, Earl of Carrick, Baron of Renfew, Lord of the Isles and Great Steward of Scotland. We would address him as "Your Royal Highness", but I suspect to William and Harry he is "Daddy".'

Nicky Gumbel

God writes with a pen that never blots, speaks with a tongue that never slips, and acts with a hand that never fails.

When God measures a man, he puts the tape around the heart instead of the head.

God is more interested in making us what he wants us to be than giving us what we think we ought to have.

Gossip

You may talk about me all you please; I'll talk about you on my knees.

Three preachers are in a boat far from land. They decide they are going to confess their shortcomings.

One asks another, 'What is something that you have a problem with?'

The first one says, 'Well, I have a problem with alcohol. I like to take to the bottle sometimes.'

The second one says, 'Well, I have a problem with lust. I desire every woman I see.'

One of the others asks the third one, 'Well, what is something that you have a problem with?'

The third preacher replies, 'Gossip, and I can't wait to get back to the shore!'

A gossip is a person with a keen sense of rumour.

Not everyone repeats gossip. Some people improve it.

Grace

A country preacher decided to skip services one Sunday and head to the hills to do some bear hunting. As he rounded the corner on a perilous twist in the trail, he and a bear collided, sending him and his rifle tumbling down the mountainside. Before he knew it, his rifle went one way and he went the other, landing on a rock and breaking both legs. That was the good news. The bad news was the ferocious bear charging at him from a distance, and he couldn't move.

'Oh, Lord,' the preacher prayed, 'I'm so sorry for skipping services today to come out here and hunt. Please forgive me and grant me just one wish… please make a Christian out of that bear that's coming at me. Please, Lord!'

That very instant, the bear skidded to a halt, fell to its knees, clasped its paws together and began to pray aloud right at the preacher's feet.

'Dear God, bless this food I am about to receive….'

Greed

According to the United Nations' Human Development Report 1996, the combined wealth of the world's 358 billionnaires now equals the total income of the poorest forty-five percent of the world's population, some 2.3 billion people.

The Yuppies' creed: I want it all, and I want it now.

Heaven

The poem is from the *Westminster Gazette* during the First World War:

They left the fury of the fight,
And they were tired.
The gates of heaven were open quite,
Unguarded and unwired.

There was no sound of any gun,
The land was still and green.
Wide hills lay silent in the sun,
Blue valleys slept between.

They saw far off a little wood,
Stand up against the sky.
Knee deep in grass a great tree stood,
Some lazy cows went by.

There were some rooks sailed overhead,
And once a church bell pealed.
'God, but it's England!' someone said,
'And there's a cricket field.'

Anon

There are many people whose faith is not strong enough to get them to church, yet they expect that it will be strong enough to get them to heaven.

'If you want to get to heaven, then you have to travel via King's Cross.'

J. John

SCENE:	The pearly gates to heaven. St Peter is receptionist at the entrance.

A cat shows up.

ST PETER:	I know you! You were a very nice cat on earth and didn't cause any trouble, so I want to offer a gift to you of one special thing you have always wanted.
CAT:	Well, I did always long to own a nice satin pillow like my master had, so I could lie on it.
ST PETER:	That's easy. Granted. You shall have the satin pillow after you enter in.

Next a group of mice appear.

ST PETER:	Ah, I remember you. You were such good mice on earth. You didn't steal food from anyone's house and never hurt other animals. Therefore, I want to grant you one special wish you always wanted.
THE CHIEF MOUSE:	Well, we always watched the children playing and saw them roller skate, and it was beautiful, and it looked like so much fun. So can we each have some roller skates, please?
ST PETER:	Granted. You shall have your wish.

Next day, St Peter is making the rounds inside the gates, and sees the cat.

ST PETER:	Well, Cat…Did you enjoy the satin pillow?
CAT:	Oh, indeed I did. And I say, that 'meals on wheels' thing was a nice touch, too!

Hell

A man was driving to work when a lorry drove through a stop sign, hit his car broadside, and knocked him out. Passers-by pulled him from the wreck and revived him. He began a terrific struggle and had to be tranquillised by the medics.

Later, when he was calm, they asked him why he struggled so. He said, 'I remember the impact, then nothing. I woke up on a concrete slab in front of a huge, flashing "Shell" sign. And somebody was standing in front of the S.'

Helpfulness

His name was Fleming, and he was a poor Scottish farmer. One day, while trying to make a living for his family, he heard a cry for help coming from a nearby bog. He dropped his tools and ran to the bog. There, mired to his waist in black muck, was a terrified boy, screaming and struggling to free himself. Farmer Fleming saved the lad from what would have been a slow and terrifying death.

The next day, a fancy carriage pulled up at the Scotsman's sparse surroundings. An elegantly dressed nobleman stepped out and introduced himself as the boy's father. 'I want to repay you,' said the nobleman. 'You saved my son's life.' 'No, I can't accept payment for what I did,' said the Scottish farmer, waving off the offer.

At that moment the farmer's own son came to the door of the family hovel. 'Is that your son?' the nobleman asked. 'Yes,' the farmer replied proudly. 'I'll make you a deal. Let me take him and give him a good education. If the lad is anything like his father, he'll grow to be a man you can be proud of.' And that he did.

In time, farmer Fleming's son graduated from St Mary's Hospital Medical School in London, and went on to become known throughout the world as the noted Sir Alexander Fleming, the discoverer of Penicillin. Years afterwards, the nobleman's son was stricken with pneumonia. What saved him? Penicillin. The name of the nobleman? Lord Randolph Churchill. His son's name? Sir Winston Churchill!

A priest is walking down the street one day when he notices a very small boy trying to press a doorbell on a house across the street. However, the boy is very short and the doorbell is too high for him to reach. After watching the boy's efforts for some time, the priest moves closer to the boy's position. He steps smartly across the street, walks up behind the little fellow and, placing his hand kindly on the child's shoulder, leans over and gives the doorbell a solid ring. Crouching down to the child's level, the priest smiles benevolently and asks,

'And now what, my little man?'

To which the boy replies, 'Now we run!'

Howlers

Newspaper headlines of 1998

1. Include Your Children When Baking Cookies

2. Something Went Wrong in Jet Crash, Experts Say

3. Typhoon Rips through Cemetery; Hundreds Dead

4. Iraqi Head Seeks Arms

5. Prostitutes Appeal to Pope

6. Panda Mating Fails; Veterinarian Takes Over

7. Miners Refuse to Work After Death

8. Stolen Painting Found by Tree

9. War Dims Hope for Peace

10. If Strike Isn't Settled Quickly, It May Last a While

11. Couple Slain; Police Suspect Homicide

12. Kids Make Nutritious Snacks

13. Survivor of Siamese Twins Joins Parents

14. Hospitals Are Sued by Seven Foot Doctors

15. Enraged Cow Injures Farmer with Axe

The following are ACTUAL answers given by contestants on *Family Fortunes* in the UK.

Q. Name a bird with a long neck.
A. Naomi Campbell.

Q. Name an occupation where you
   need a torch.
A. A burglar.

Q. Name a famous brother and sister.
A. Bonnie and Clyde.

Q. Name an item of clothing worn by
   the Three Musketeers.
A. A horse.

Q. Name something that floats in the
   bath.
A. Water.

Q. Name something you wear on the
   beach.
A. A deckchair.

Q. Name something red.
A. My cardigan.

Q. Name a famous royal.
A. Mail.

Q. Name something that flies that
   doesn't have an engine.
A. A bicycle with wings.

Q. Name something you might be
   allergic to.
A. Skiing.

Q. Name a famous bridge.
A. The bridge over troubled waters.

Q. Name something a cat does.
A. Goes to the toilet.

Q. Name something you do in the
   bathroom.
A. Decorate.

Q. Name an animal you might see at
   the zoo.
A. A dog.

Q. Name something associated with
   the police.
A. Pigs.

Q. Name a sign of the zodiac.
A. April.

Q. Name something slippery.
A. A conman.

Q. Name a jacket potato topping.
A. Jam.

Q. Name a famous Scotsman.
A. Jock.

Q. Name something with a hole in it.
A. Window.

Q. Name a non-living object with legs.
A. Plant.

Q. Name a domestic animal.
A. Leopard.

Q. Name a part of the body beginning
   with 'N'.
A. Knee.

Q. Name a way of cooking fish.
A. Cod.

Q. Name something you open other
   than a door.
A. Your bowels.

Here are some signs and notices written in English that were actually discovered throughout the world.

Outside a Hong Kong tailor shop: Ladies may have a fit upstairs.

In a Bangkok dry cleaner's: Drop your trousers here for best results.

In a Tokyo hotel: Is forbidden to steal hotel towels please. If you are not a person to do such thing is please not to read notice.

In an advertisement by a Hong Kong dentist: Teeth extracted by the latest Methodists.

In a Rome laundry: Ladies, leave your clothes here and spend the afternoon having a good time.

Advertisement for donkey rides in Thailand: Would you like to ride on your own ass?

From a Japanese information booklet about using a hotel air conditioner: Cooles and Heates — if you want just condition of warm in your room, please control yourself.

In a Bucharest hotel lobby: The lift is being fixed for the next day. During that time we regret that you will be unbearable.

In a Paris hotel elevator: Please leave your values at the front desk.

In a hotel in Athens: Visitors are expected to complain at the office between the hours of 9 and 11 am daily.

In a Yugoslavian hotel: The flattening of underwear with pleasure is the job of the chambermaid.

In a Japanese hotel: You are invited to take advantage of the chambermaid.

In the lobby of a Moscow hotel across from a Russian Orthodox monastery: You are welcome to visit the cemetery where famous Russian and Soviet composers, artists and writers are buried daily except Thursday.

On the menu of a Swiss restaurant: Our wines leave you nothing to hope for.

A sign posted in Germany's Black Forest: It is strictly forbidden on our Black Forest camping site that people of different sex, for instance, men and women, live together in one tent unless they are married with each other for that purpose.

In a Zurich hotel: Because of the impropriety of entertaining guests of the opposite sex in the bedroom, it is suggested that the lobby be used for this purpose.

In a Copenhagen airline ticket office: We take your bags and send them in all directions.

In a Budapest zoo: Please do not feed the animals. If you have any suitable food, give it to the guard on duty.

In the office of a Roman doctor: Specialist in women and other diseases.

In an Acapulco hotel: The manager has personally passed all the water served here.

The following extracts are perfectly genuine — taken from actual letters sent to the DHSS (Social Security). Although rather crude they are written in good faith by the senders:

Our lavatory seat is broken in half and is now in three pieces.

Can you please tell me when our repairs are going to be done as my wife is about to become an expectant mother.

The toilet is blocked and we can't bath the children until it is cleared.

Will you please send someone to mend our broken path as my wife tripped and fell on it and she is now pregnant.

Our kitchen floor is very damp and we have two children and we would like a third so will you please send somebody round to do something about it.

Mrs Smith has no clothes and has had none for over a year. The clergy have been visiting her.

I am pleased to inform you that my husband who was reported missing, is dead.

Mrs Adams has asked me to collect her money as she is going in to hospital to have her overtures out.

Unless I get my husband's maintenance money soon I shall be obliged to live an immortal life.

The children have been off school because there is a lot of measles about and I had them humanised.

You have changed my little boy into a little girl. Will this matter?

Mrs Brown only THINKS she's ill, but believe me she is nothing but a hypodermic.

In accordance with your instructions I have given birth to twins in the enclosed envelope.

I want my sick pay. I've been in bed under the doctor for a week and he's doing me no good. If things don't improve I'll get another doctor.

Milk is wanted for my baby and the father is unable to supply it.

Re: your dental enquiry. The teeth on top are all right but those on my bottom are hurting dreadfully.

I am very annoyed to find you have branded my son illiterate. This is a lie as I married his father a week before he was born.

This is to let you know there is a smell coming from the man next door.

The milkman provides a flexible service and is able to respond to his customer's varying milk requirements if they leave him a note. However, not all the notes are as simple as 'one extra pint please'. Often they can be very amusing as the following selection illustrates.

There was the note left out by a housewife for her milkman reading:

**Dear Milkman,
Just had a baby. Please leave another one.**

Other classic notes include:

Please leave an extra pint of paralysed.

Please cancel one pint after the day after today.

Milkman. Please close the gate behind you because the birds keep pecking the tops off the milk.

No milk. Please do not leave milk at Number 14 as he is dead until further notice.

Please leave no milk today. When I say today, I mean tomorrow, for I wrote this note yesterday.

Leave one extra pint. If this note blows away, please knock.

Please knock. My TV has broken down and I missed last night's *Coronation Street*. If you saw it, will you tell me what happened.

No milk, thank you. We are away for the weekend — which is why I am hiding this note under the doormat so that nobody finds out.

Sorry not to have paid your bill before, but my wife had a baby and I have been carrying it around in my pocket for weeks.

From now on please leave two pints every other day and one pint on the days in between — except Wednesdays and Saturdays when I don't want any milk.

Please send me a form of cheap milk for I am stagnant.

Milk is needed for the baby. Father is unable to supply it.

And finally a note left for Nigel Matthew, 1991 winner of Britain's Best Milkman title: Money on table, wife in bed, please help yourself.

Humanity

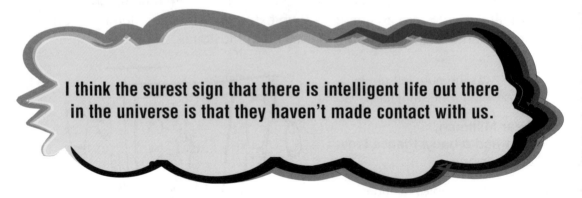

I think the surest sign that there is intelligent life out there in the universe is that they haven't made contact with us.

Humility

> Religion says, 'Be good, conform yourself.'
> Epicureanism says, 'Be sensuous, satisfy yourself.'
> Education says, 'Be resourceful, expand yourself.'
> Psychology says, 'Be confident, assert yourself.'
> Materialism says, 'Be possessive, please yourself.'
> Ascetism says, 'Be lowly, suppress yourself.'
> Humanism says, 'Be capable, believe in yourself.'
> Pride says, 'Be superior, promote yourself.'
> Christ says, 'Be unselfish, humble yourself.'
>
> **Chuck Swindoll**

'Everything in God's store is on the bottom shelf… you have to get on your knees to get it.'

Robert Collier

I

Identity

A Swedish bishop was coming to the end of his ministry. It was decided it was time to paint his portrait for the gallery of bishops in the palace. The diocese rather bravely decided to commission a modern artist. He painted the portrait and then the great day of unveiling arrived. The painting was uncovered in front of the bishop and a group of dignitaries. Everyone went quiet. On the canvas were hundreds of abstract patterns, colours, shapes and the vague outline of a head right at the centre.

'Bishop, what do you think?' they asked.

He replied, 'Matthew 14.27 — "Take heart, be not afraid, it is I."'

Incarnation

A Jewish father was troubled by the way his son turned out, and went to see his rabbi about it.

'I brought him up in the faith, gave him a very expensive bar mitzvah, cost me a fortune to educate him. Then he tells me last week he has decided to be a Christian! Rabbi, where did I go wrong?'

'Funny you should come to me,' said the rabbi. 'Like you I, too, brought my boy up in the faith, put him through university, cost me a fortune, then one day he, too, tells me he has decided to become a Christian.'

'What did you do?' asked the father.

'I turned to God for the answer,' replied the rabbi.

'And what did he say?' pressed the father.

'God said, "Funny you should come to me."'

'Like a stone on the surface of a still river, driving the ripples on for ever, redemption rips through the surface of time, in the cry of a tiny babe.'
Bruce Cockburn, from his 1991 album — *Nothing but a Burning Light*

History is littered with examples of men who would become gods, but only one example of God becoming man.

Independence

A man injured on the job filed an insurance claim. The insurance company requested more information, so the man wrote the insurance company the following letter of explanation:

Dear Sirs

I am writing in response to your request concerning clarification of the information I supplied on the insurance form which asked for the cause of the injury. I answered, 'Trying to do the job alone.' I trust that the following explanation will be sufficient.

I am a bricklayer by trade. On the date of the injury I was working alone laying brick around the top of a three-storey building. When I finished the job I had about 500lbs of brick left over. Rather than carry the bricks down by hand I decided to put them into a barrel and lower them by a pulley that was fastened to the top of the building.

I secured the end of the rope at ground level, went back up to the top of the building, loaded the bricks into the barrel and pushed it over the side. I then went back down to the ground and untied the rope holding it securely to ensure the slow descent of the barrel. I weigh 145lbs. At the shock of being jerked off the ground so swiftly by the 500lbs of bricks in the barrel, I lost my presence of mind and forgot to let go of the rope.

Between the second and third floors I met the barrel. This accounts for the bruises and lacerations on my upper body. Fortunately I retained enough presence of mind to maintain my tight hold on the rope and proceeded rapidly up the side of the building, not stopping until my right hand was jammed in the pulley. This accounts for my broken thumb. Despite the pain, I continued to hold tightly to the rope. Unfortunately at approximately the same time the barrel hit the ground the bottom fell out of the barrel. Devoid of the weight of the bricks, the barrel now weighed about 50lbs. I began a rapid descent.

In the vicinity of the second floor, I met the barrel coming up. This explains the injury to my legs and lower body. Slowed only slightly, I continued my descent landing on the pile of bricks. Fortunately my back was only sprained. I am sorry to report however that at this point I again lost my presence of mind and let go of the rope.

I trust this answers your concern. Please note that I am finished trying to do the job alone.

Inheritance

There was once a very successful businessman who had an only son. The man cherished the child and longed to find a way to express his deep love so he decided that each year he would purchase a priceless, multi-million dollar painting that captured the real sentiments of his heart. He would hang that year's painting over the huge fireplace hearth in the most prominent place of the house.

For the first several years the father chose the painting himself as his son was too young. The first year he selected a glorious sunrise depicting the radiance of life that his son had brought. The next was a mountain stream showing the refreshing overflow of love they had together. The third year, as his son began to learn about God as creator, he bought a magnificent canvas of a grand mountain scene. As the son matured he began to help the father choose the paintings until they owned one of the most valuable collections in the world.

One day war broke out in the land and the son was drafted. He met a young man who would become his dearest, most loyal friend. This friend turned out to be a delightful amateur artist who drew a simple but eloquent sketch of the son shortly before the son was killed in battle. At the funeral the friend presented the modest, obviously amateur drawing to the father describing what his son had meant to him during his rigorous military days. The father hung the picture over the mantle in the place of honour above the rest of the priceless paintings they had collected.

A few years later the father died and the collection was auctioned to the highest bidder. Art curators from around the world descended upon the home hoping to purchase any or all of the paintings. The room was electric with anticipation as the auctioneer opened the bidding at $1000 for the amateur drawing of the son. 'Do I hear a $1000 for the son? Do I hear $500? $200? Who will have the son?' he begged. Finally, a buyer purchased the sketch so that they could move on with the 'real' collection.

Then the auctioneer did the unthinkable. He ordered the auction closed! Hundreds of buyers gasped with disbelief — 'How can this be? We have come from around the world. How dare you cut us off.' The auctioneer regained order and explained. 'It was the father's desire that the entire collection be given to the one who buys the simple sketch of his son! For whoever has his son has his all!'

Insults

Once there was a disciple of a renowned Greek philosopher who was handed an odd assignment. He was commanded by his master to give money to everyone who insulted him, for a period of three years. Wanting very much to awaken, this student did exactly what he was told.

When this rather lengthy trial was over, the master summoned the young man to his quarters and said to him: 'Now you can go to Athens, for you are ready to learn wisdom.'

Elated, the disciple set off for Athens. Just before he entered the great city, he saw a certain wise man sitting at the gate insulting everybody who came and went. Naturally, the moment this fellow saw the disciple he insulted him, too.

'Hey!' he cried out to the student, 'How did you get to be so ugly and stupid? I have never before seen anyone as ridiculous looking as you.'

But instead of taking offence, the disciple just burst out laughing.

'Why do you laugh when I insult you?' asked the wise man.

'Because,' said the disciple, 'for three whole years I have been paying for this kind of thing and now you give it to me for NOTHING!'

'Enter the city,' said the wise man. 'It is all yours.'

Intelligence

'The test of a first-rate intelligence is the ability to hold two opposed ideas in the mind at the same time and still retain the ability to function.' **F Scott Fitzgerald**

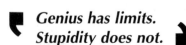 *Genius has limits. Stupidity does not.*

Don't always assume the other person has equal intelligence — they might have more.

The only reason some people are lost in thought is because they're total strangers there.

In a recent issue of *Meat and Poultry* magazine, editors quoted from *Feathers*, the publication of the California Poultry Industry Federation, telling the following story:

It seems the US Federal Aviation Administration has a unique device for testing the strength of windshields on airplanes. The device is a gun that launches a dead chicken at a plane's windshield at approximately the speed the plane flies. The theory is that if the windshield doesn't crack from the carcass impact, it'll survive a real collision with a bird during flight. It seems the British were very interested in this and wanted to test a windshield on a brand new, speedy locomotive they're developing. They borrowed the FAA's chicken launcher, loaded the chicken and fired. The ballistic chicken shattered the windshield, went through the engineer's chair, broke an instrument panel and embedded itself in the back wall of the engine cab. The British were stunned and asked the FAA to recheck the test to see if everything was done correctly. The FAA reviewed the test thoroughly and had one recommendation: 'Use a thawed chicken.'

Intercession

When a maid in a large house retired for the night she would always pick up the newspaper that the master had finished reading. The master was intrigued by this and wanted to know what she looked at and what interested her in the paper. One day the master asked her. She said, 'I read the births, deaths and marriages.' He asked her why. She said, 'So that I can pray for all the children that are born into this world who need God to protect them. I pray that they will grow up knowing God. I pray for all those who are mourning their lost ones and I pray that they will find comfort in the shepherd, and I pray for all those who are being married that they will know something of the sanctity of holy marriage.'

Webster's definition of intercession: To intervene between parties with a view to reconciling differences. Synonym: mediate.

Intercession is love on its knees working with God.

J

Jesus

Jesus and Satan have an argument as to who is the better computer programmer. This goes on for a few hours until they come to an agreement to hold a contest, with God as the judge. They set themselves before their computers and begin. They type furiously, lines of code streaming up the screen, for several hours on end.

Seconds before the end of the competition, a bolt of lightning strikes, taking out the electricity. Moments later, the power is restored, and God announces that the contest is over. He asks Satan to show what he has come up with. Satan is visibly upset and cries, 'I have nothing. I lost it all when the power went out.'

'Very well, then,' says God, 'let us see if Jesus fared any better.'

Jesus enters a command, and the screen comes to life in vivid display, the voices of an angelic choir pour forth from the speakers.

Satan is astonished. He exclaims, 'But how? I lost everything, yet Jesus' programme is intact! How did he do it?'

God chuckles, 'Everybody knows… Jesus saves.'

Quotes from non-Christian historians of Jesus' time:

Josephus:

Now there was about this time Jesus, a wise man, if it be lawful to call him a man, for he was a doer of wonderful works a teacher of such men as receive the truth with pleasure. He drew over to him both many of the Jews, and many of the Gentiles. He was [the] Christ. And when Pilate, at the suggestion of the principal men among us, had condemned him to the cross, those that loved him at the first did not forsake him; for he appeared to them alive again the third day; as the divine prophets had foretold these and ten thousand other wonderful things concerning him. And the tribe of Christians so named from him are not extinct at this day.

Josephus, 'Antiquities' XVIII, iii, 3.
See Philip Schaff,
History of the Christian Church
(Michigan: Eerdmans, 1950),
Vol. 1, pp.92ff.

Tacitus:

But not all the relief that could come from man, not all the bounties that the prince could bestow, nor all the atonements which could be presented to the gods, availed to relieve Nero from the infamy of being believed to have ordered the conflagration. Hence, to suppress the rumour, he falsely charged with the guilt, and punished with the most exquisite tortures, the persons commonly called Christians, who were hated for their enormities. Christus, the founder of that name, was put to death as a criminal by Pontius Pilate, procurator of Judea in the reign of Tiberius: but the pernicious superstition, repressed for a time, broke out again, not only through Judea, where the mischief originated, but through the city of Rome.

Tacitus, 'Annals' xv, 44.
The Oxford Translation, Revised
(New York: Harper and Bros.,
Publishers, 1858), p. 423.

Pliny:

They [the Christians] affirmed, however, the whole of their guilt, or their error, was, that they were in the habit of meeting on a certain fixed day before it was light, when they sang in alternate verses a hymn to Christ, as to a god, and bound themselves by a solemn oath, not to any wicked deeds, but never to commit any fraud, theft or adultery, never to falsify their word, nor to deny a trust when they should be called on to deliver it up.

Pliny, 'Letters' X, xcvi. Loeb Classical Library. English translation by William Melmoth, revised by WML Hutchinson (London: William Heinemann; Cambridge, Mass.: Harvard University Press, 1935), Vol. II, p.103.

Lucian:

… the man who was crucified in Palestine because he introduced this new cult into the world… Furthermore, their first lawgiver persuaded them that they are all brothers one of another after they have transgressed once for all by denying the Greek gods and by worshipping that crucified sophist himself and living under his laws.

Lucian, 'The Passing of Peregrinus' 12, 13. Loeb Classical Library. English translation by AM Harmon (London: William Heinemann Ltd.; Cambridge, Mass.: Harvard University Press, 1936), pp.13, 15.

Not long ago, an elderly Pentecostal statesman (Dr Lockeridge) was spotted in the crowd at a conference and asked to come up to the platform and open proceedings with a spontaneous prayer. This is a transcript of what he said:

The Bible says my king is a seven-way king:
He's the king of the Jews — that's a racial king.
He's the king of Israel — that's a national king.
He's the king of righteousness.
He's the king of the ages.
He's the king of heaven.
He's the king of glory.
He's the king of kings and he's the Lord of lords.
That's my king.
… Well, I wonder, do you know him?

David said, 'The heavens declare the glory of God and the firmament showeth his handiwork.'
My king is a sovereign king — no means of measure can define his limitless love.
No farseeing telescope can bring into visibility the coastline of his shoreless supplies.
No barrier can hinder him from pouring out his blessings.
He's enduringly strong.
He's entirely sincere.
He's eternally steadfast.
He's immortally graceful.
He's imperially powerful.
He's impartially merciful… Do you know Him?

He's the greatest phenomenon that has ever crossed the horizon of this world.
He's God's Son.
He's the sinner's Saviour.
He's the centrepiece of civilisation.
He stands in the solitude of himself.
He's august and he's unique.
He's unparalleled, he's unprecedented.
He's the loftiest idea in literature.
He's the highest personality in philosophy.
He is the supreme problem in higher criticism.
He's the fundamental doctrine of true theology.
He's the core and necessity for spiritual religion.
He's the miracle of the age, yes, he is.

He's the superlative of everything good that you choose to call him.
He's the only one qualified to be an all-sufficient Saviour.
… I wonder if you know him today?

He supplies strength for the weak.
He's available for the tempted and the tried.

He sympathises and he saves.
He strengthens and sustains.
He guards and he guides.
He heals the sick.
He cleanses the lepers.
He forgives sinners.
He discharges debtors.
He delivers the captives.
He defends the feeble.
He blesses the young.
He serves the unfortunate.
He regards the aged.
He rewards the diligent and
He beautifies the meek.
… I wonder if you know him?

Well, this is my king.
He is the king!
He's the key to knowledge.
He's the wellspring of wisdom.
He's the doorway of
deliverance.
He's the pathway of peace.
He's the roadway of
righteousness.
He's the highway of holiness.
He's the gateway of glory.
… Do you know him?

Well, his office is manifold.
His promise is sure.
His life is matchless.
His goodness is limitless.
His mercy is everlasting.
His love never changes.
His word is enough.
His grace is sufficient.
His reign is righteous and
His yoke is easy and
His burden is light.

I wish I could describe him to you.
But he's indescribable — Yea! Yea! Yea!
He's indescribable — Yes he is! He's God.
He's indescribable.
He's incomprehensible.
He's invincible.
He's irresistible!

Well, you can't get him out of your mind.
You can't get him off of your hand.
You can't outlive him and
You can't live without him.

Well, the Pharisees couldn't stand him, but they found out they couldn't stop him.
Pilate couldn't find any fault in him.
The witnesses couldn't get their testimonies to agree.
Herod couldn't kill him.
Death couldn't handle him and
The grave couldn't hold Him. Yea!
That's my king!
That's my king! Yea!

And thine is the kingdom and the power and the glory for ever and ever and ever and ever.
How long is that?
And ever and ever.
And when you get through all the for evers, then Amen!

GOOD GOD ALMIGHTY! AMEN! AMEN!

There was once a man who lived during a precisely defined period in the reigns of Augustus and Tiberias Caesar. His existence is an incontestable fact. He was known as a manual worker, a carpenter using the hammer and the plane, with shavings curling round his ears. He could be seen walking along a road which is still pointed out to us; in the evening he would be stretched upon a bed of rushes or a string hammock, tired out and sleeping like any other man ,just like one of us. Yet he said the most surprising things that have ever been heard.

He said that he was the Messiah, the heaven-sent witness through whom the chosen people were to fulfil their glorious destiny. More astounding still, he said he was the Son of God. And he was believed. He found men to accompany him along the roads of Palestine, as he travelled across the country. He performed miracles with disconcerting ease. There were many who believed that he would bring about the political independence of Israel.

But then, any mystic can collect devoted fanatics. The culmination of this scandal was that the man was suddenly wiped out, without putting up the slightest resistance. So far from being discouraged by this failure, several of his disciples went out into the world to bear witness to his divinity, even with their blood, and ever since humankind, seeing in this defeat the sign of victory, has prostrated itself before a common gibbet, just as if tomorrow a church should raise the scaffold for the veneration of the crowd.

Jesus is at once of history and beyond it. Considering the number and the agreement of the witnesses concerning him and the abundance of the written testimony through which his gospel has been transmitted, one is inclined to say that there is no individual of his time about whom we are so well informed. Yet as he himself foretold he has become the centre of a thousand years of dispute, which each generation renews in contemporary terms.

That this man of poor and uncultivated stock should remake the basis of philosophy and open out to the world of the future an unknown territory of thought; that this simple son of a declining people, born in an obscure district in a small Roman province, this nameless Jew like all those others despised by the procurators of Caesar, should speak with a voice that was to sound above those of the emperors' themselves, these are the most surprising facts of history.

Hence forward he is the measure of everything that happens. The life of Christ is contained in history and contains it. It is not merely the vindication of some nameless tragic humility, it is the supreme explanation and the final standard by which everything is measured, from which history itself takes meaning and justification.'

Daniel Rops, *Jesus And His Times,* translated from the French by Ruby Miller (New York: E P Dutton and Co., INC, 1954), pp.11-13.

Judaism

In the Middle Ages, the Pope decided that all the Jews had to leave Rome. Naturally there was a big uproar from the Jewish community. So the Pope made a deal. He would have a religious debate with a member of the Jewish community. If the Jew won, the Jews could stay. If the Pope won, the Jews would leave.

The Jews realised that they had no choice. They looked around for a champion who could defend their faith, but no one wanted to volunteer. It was too risky. So they finally picked an old man named Moishe, who spent his life sweeping up after people, to represent them. Being old and poor he had less to lose, so he agreed. He asked only for one addition to the debate. Not being used to saying very much as he cleaned up around the settlement, he asked that neither side be allowed to talk. The Pope agreed.

The day of the great debate came. Moishe and the Pope sat opposite each other for a full minute before the Pope raised his hand and showed three fingers. Moishe looked back at him and raised one finger. The Pope waved his fingers in a circle around his head. Moishe pointed to the ground where he sat. The Pope pulled out a wafer and a glass of wine. Moishe pulled out an apple. The Pope stood up and said, 'I give up. This man is too good. The Jews can stay.'

An hour later, the cardinals were all around the Pope asking him what happened. The Pope said: 'First I held up three fingers to represent the Trinity. He responded by holding up one finger to remind me that there was still one God common to both our religions. Then I waved my finger around me to show him, that God was all around us. He responded by pointing to the ground, showing that God was also right here with us. I pulled out the wine and the wafer to show that God absolves us from our sins. He pulled out an apple to remind me of original sin. He had an answer for everything. What could I do?'

Meanwhile, the Jewish community had crowded around Moishe, amazed that this old, almost feeble-minded man had done what all their scholars had insisted was impossible! 'What happened?' they asked. 'Well,' said Moishe, 'First he said to me that the Jews had three days to get out of here. I told him that not one of us was leaving. Then he told me that this whole city would be cleared of Jews. I let him know that we were staying right here.' 'And then?' asked a woman. 'I don't know,' said Moishe. 'He took out his lunch and I took out mine.'

Leadership

To be a leader is to be vulnerable — to meet the disapproving stares of others with the joy and certainty of God's infinite love;

To be a leader is to be imperfect — to enjoy the enriching process of a new challenge with the hope and confidence of the master;

To be a leader is to be naive — to believe the very best of all people in the love and acceptance of our Saviour;

To be a leader is to be trusting — to disregard dire projections of gloom for the joy and creativity of our creator;

To be a leader is to be honest — to own our sinfulness with the sincerity and authenticity of the Spirit;

To be a leader is to be unique — to accept the wonderful gift of self, in the knowledge and understanding of community;

To be a leader is to be free — to welcome recurring waves of change with the awe and wonder of a child;

To be a leader is to be empowering — to share the exhilarating power of information in the establishment of inter-connectedness;

To be a leader is to be humble — to give the inestimable gift of flexibility with the grace and forgiveness of God;

To be a leader is to be whole — to know the startling reality that I am central, yet peripheral, in God's plan for the world;

To be a leader is to be weak — to understand that I can rest in the hollow of God's hand only in the total yielding and complete trusting of my child's heart.

Dee Bernhardt

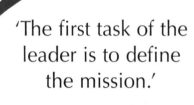

'The first task of the leader is to define the mission.'

Peter F Drucker

A leader does the right thing. A manager does the thing right.

Anyone can steer the ship when the sea is calm.

'Either lead, follow or get out of the way.'

Ted Turner

Leaders create energy in others by distilling purpose.

A truly great leader is someone who never allows their followers to discover that they are as ignorant as they are.

'Example has more
followers than reason.'

Christian Bovee

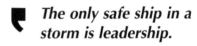 *The only safe ship in a
storm is leadership.*

**Sometimes the best helping
hand you can give is a good
firm push.**

 What this country needs is more leaders who know what this
country needs.

Legacy

Sarah Edwards was the wife of the most famous revival preacher
in US history, Jonathan Edwards (eighteenth century). She was a
mother of eleven. Out of their 1,400 descendants, the family
produced:

> 13 college presidents
> 65 professors
> 100 lawyers and a dean of a law school
> 30 judges
> 66 physicians
> 80 public office holders, including
> > 3 mayors
> > 3 governors
> > 3 US senators
> > a controller of the US treasury
> > a vice-president of the US

Lent

Fast from judging others;
Feast on Christ dwelling in them.

Fast from emphasis on differences;
Feast on the unity of all life.

Fast from apparent darkness;
Feast on the reality of all light.

Fast from thoughts of illness;
Feast on the healing power of
     God.

Fast from words that pollute;
Feast on phrases that purify.

Fast from discontent;
Feast on gratitude.

Fast from anger;
Feast on patience.

Fast from pessimism;
Feast on optimism.

Fast from worry;
Feast on God's providence.

Fast from complaining;
Feast on appreciation.

Fast from negatives;
Feast on affirmatives.

Fast from unrelenting pressures;
Feast on unceasing prayer.

Fast from hostility;
Feast on non-resistance.

Fast from bitterness;
Feast on forgiveness.

Fast from self-concern;
Feast on compassion for others.

Fast from personal anxiety;
Feast on eternal truth.

Fast from discouragement;
Feast on hope.

Fast from facts that depress;
Feast on verities that uplift.

Fast from lethargy;
Feast on enthusiasm.

Fast from suspicion;
Feast on truth.

Fast from thoughts that weaken;
Feast on promises that inspire.

Fast from shadows of sorrow;
Feast on the sunlight of serenity.

Fast from idle gossip;
Feast on purposeful silence.

Fast from problems that
     overwhelm;
Feast on prayer that sustains.

Anon.

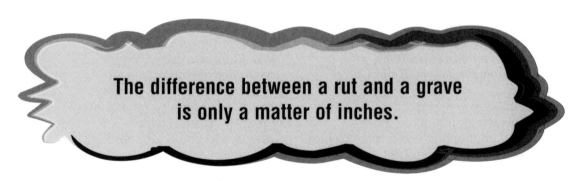

The difference between a rut and a grave is only a matter of inches.

A letter from a young person to a popular magazine sums up the life lived by many in 'Generation X' today:

I've been dropping pills for ages and it really has reached the stage when all that seems pointless. I've noticed such a change in my own life since I started puffing, pilling and speeding. To say that I'm paranoid would be a huge understatement. Getting out of the cycle, however, is almost impossible. I think drugs are just another feature of 'Generation X' — another way to escape the hopelessness we view around us every day. I'm desperately searching for something to believe in, something to live for, but there's just nothing out there. The contrast between our generation and the ones which have gone before is huge. There's nothing new, everything is retrospective: fashion, music, politics — the lot. I just don't get a kick out of life, and drugs replace that. They help me forget who I am and the hopelessness which surrounds me. To address drug abuse, you need to tackle far wider issues — the general lack of enthusiasm of our generation and the fact that we don't feel we can make a difference. People say that we don't care, but it's not that. The fact is, we care too much but can't see any way to alter the situation. I've had bad experiences with drugs, pills especially — but until I can find something else worth while in life I'll carry on taking them to escape and get my kicks. I challenge you to make life worth while and to create something new.

Signed BERI

Lifestyle

If Jesus Christ came to your house
To spend a day or two,
If he came unexpectedly
I wonder what you'd do?

I know you'd give the nicest room
To such an honoured guest
And all the food you'd serve to him
Would be the very best.

You'd keep on reassuring him
You were glad to have him there,
That serving him in your own home
Is joy beyond compare.

But when you saw him coming
Would your welcome be sincere,
Or deep down would you worry
That this man had come too near?

Or would you have a change of
     clothes
Before you let him in
Or hide some magazines
And put a Bible where they'd been?

Would you turn off the video
And hope he had not seen
The picture that was showing
On your Nicam TV screen?

Would you hide your world of
     music,
Tuck your CDs out of sight?
Would you rush about and tidy
Other things that were not right?

I wonder if the Saviour
Spent a day or two with you
Would you choose to keep on doing
All those things you often do?

Would you choose to keep on saying
All those things you often say?
Would life for you continue
As it does from day to day?

Would your family conversation lull
Or keep its usual pace
And would you find it hard each
     meal
To say a table grace?

Would you sing the songs you
     always sing?
And read the books you read
And let him know the things
On which your mind and spirit feed?

Would you take Jesus with you
Everywhere you plan to go
Or would you maybe change your
     plans
For just a day or so?

Would you be glad to have him
Meet your very closest friends
Or would you hope they'd stay away
Until his visit ends?

Would you be glad to have him
Stay for ever, on and on
Or would you sigh with great relief
When he at last was gone?

It might be interesting to know
The things that you would do
If Jesus came in person
And spent some time with you.

Anon.

Loneliness

'I've felt incredible loneliness in my life. I've known great despair. And what is the point of having a great job or something spectacular happening if you have no one to share it with? Unless you have someone, it's pointless. It's vapour.'

Julia Roberts

'All the money and all the fame in the world is worth nothing if you're lonely.'

Tom Cruise

Longevity

A man once advised his son that if he wanted to live a long life, the secret was to sprinkle a little gunpowder on his corn flakes every morning.

The son did this religiously, and he lived to the age of ninety-three. When he died, he left fourteen children, twenty-eight grandchildren, thirty-five great-grandchildren, and a fifteen-foot hole in the wall of the crematorium.

Love

A child psychologist moved into a new neighbourhood. He had a particularly irritating habit of correcting parents in the estate for their bad parenting. If he saw something he didn't like, he would come out of his house and say to the parent, 'That's not the way, love's the way, love's the way.' After a few months of this, the local residents were getting decidedly annoyed. One day, the child psychologist was laying a new path in front of his house. A teenager came careering down the street on his BMX bike but lost control and went ploughing through the wet cement. The child psychologist, in a fit of rage, cuffed the boy on the ear. His mother, watching from her kitchen window, jumped for joy. She dashed out of her house, looked the psychologist in the eye, and said, 'That's not the way; love's the way, love's the way.' To which the child psychologist replied, 'Ah yes, but I was talking about love in the abstract, not in the concrete!'

A preacher made a statement in Hyde Park. 'You must love the Lord your God with all your heart.' A heckler replied, 'That's rubbish. Science has proved that the human heart is just a pump.'

The preacher asked, 'Are you married?' The man said, 'Yes.' 'Then go home and tell your wife you love her with all your pump!'

Dr Robert Seizer, in his book *Mortal Lessons: Notes in the Art of Surgery*, tells a remarkable story of performing surgery to remove a tumour in which it was necessary to sever a facial nerve, leaving a young woman's mouth permanently twisted in palsy. In Dr Seizer's own words:

> Her young husband is in the room. He stands on the opposite side of the bed, and together they seem to dwell in the evening lamplight, isolated from me, private. Who are they, I ask myself, he and this wry-mouth I have made, who gaze at and touch each other so generously, greedily? The young woman speaks. 'Will my mouth always be like this?' She asks. 'Yes,' I say, 'it will. It is because the nerve was cut.' She nods, and is silent. But the young man smiles. 'I like it,' he says. 'It is kind of cute.' All at once I know who he is. I understand, and I lower my gaze. One is not bold in an encounter with God. Unmindful, he bends to kiss her crooked mouth, and I, so close, can see how he twists his own lips to accommodate to hers, to show her that their kiss still works.

Lying

A small boy in Sunday school was asked what a lie was. He said, 'A lie is an abomination in the eyes of God.' Then added, 'And our very present help in times of trouble!'

Manipulation

Little Leroy went to his mother demanding a new bicycle. His mother decided he should take a look at himself and the way he acts. She said, 'Leroy, it isn't Christmas and we don't have the money to just go out and buy you anything you want. So why don't you write a letter to Jesus and pray for one instead.'

After his temper tantrum his mother sent him to his room. He finally sat down to write a letter to Jesus.

Dear Jesus:
I've been a good boy this year and would appreciate a new bicycle.
Your friend,
Leroy.

Now, Leroy knew that Jesus really knew what kind of boy he was. So he ripped up the letter and decided to give it another try.

Dear Jesus:
I've been an OK boy this year and I want a new bicycle.
Yours truly,
Leroy.

Well, Leroy knew this wasn't totally honest so he tore it up and tried again.

Dear Jesus:
I've thought about being a good boy this year and can I have a bicycle?
Leroy.

Leroy looked deep down in his heart, which by the way was what his mother really wanted. He knew he had been terrible and deserved almost nothing. He crumpled up the letter, threw it in the bin and went running outside. He aimlessly wandered about, depressed because of the way he treated his parents and really considering his actions. He finally found himself in front of a Catholic church. Leroy went inside and knelt down, looking around and not knowing what he should really do. Finally he got up and began to walk out of the door, looking at all the statues. All of a sudden, he grabbed a small one and ran out the door. He went home, hid it under his bed and wrote this letter.

Jesus,
I've got your mum. If you ever want to see her again, give me a bike.
You know who.

Marriage

Here are some quotes that reflect contemporary society's cynicism about marriage:

Marriage is not a word. It is a sentence. A life sentence.

Marriage is very much like a violin; after the sweet music is over the strings are attached.

Marriage is love. Love is blind.
Marriage is an institution.
Therefore, marriage is an institution for the blind.

Marriage is an institution in which a man loses his Bachelor's Degree and the woman gets her Master's.

Marriage puts one ring on a woman's finger… and two under the man's eyes.

I never knew what real happiness was until I got married and by then it was too late.

'The trouble with some women is they get all excited about nothing — and then they marry him.'
Cher

Marriages are made in heaven. But so again, are thunder and lightning.

A man is not complete until he is married — then he is finished.

A husband is living proof that a wife can take a joke.

An archaeologist is the best husband a woman can have; the older she gets, the more interested he is in her.

Marriage is bliss. Ignorance is bliss. Ergo…

Married life is very frustrating. In the first year of marriage, the man speaks and the wife listens. In the second year, the woman speaks and the husband listens. In the third year, they both speak and the neighbours listen.

I think, therefore I am single.

'If variety is the spice of life, marriage is the big can of leftover Spam.'
Johnny Carson

'Honolulu, it's got everything. Sand for the children, sun for the wife, sharks for the wife's mother.' Ken Dodd

'If you want to sacrifice the admiration of many men for the criticism of one, go ahead, get married.'
Katharine Hepburn

'Eighty percent of married men cheat in America. The rest cheat in Europe.' Jackie Mason

Marriage is a three-ring circus: engagement ring, wedding ring and suffering.

After just a few years of marriage filled with constant arguments, a young man and his wife decided the only way to save their marriage was to try counselling. They had been at each other's throats for some time and felt that this was their last straw. When they arrived at the counsellor's office, the counsellor jumped right in and opened the floor for discussion.

'What seems to be the problem?' Immediately, the husband held his long face down without anything to say. In contrast, the wife began talking ninety miles an hour, describing all the wrongs within their marriage. After fifteen minutes of listening to the wife, the counsellor went over to her and gave her a long and lingering kiss on the mouth. Then he went and sat back down.

The wife sat speechless. The marriage counsellor looked over at the husband, who stared in disbelief. The counsellor said to the husband, 'Your wife NEEDS that at least twice a week!'

The husband scratched his head and replied, 'I can have her here on Tuesdays and Thursdays.'

An elderly widow and widower were dating for about five years. The man finally decided to ask her to marry. She immediately said 'yes'.

The next morning when he awoke, he couldn't remember what her answer was! 'Was she happy? I think so, wait, no, she looked at me in a funny way…'

After about an hour of trying to remember to no avail, he got on the telephone and gave her a call. Embarrassed, he admitted that he didn't remember her answer to the marriage proposal.

'Oh,' she said, 'I'm so glad you called. I remembered saying "yes" to someone, but I couldn't remember who it was.'

A woman who died found herself standing outside the pearly gates, being greeted by St Peter. She asked him, 'Oh, is this place what I really think it is? It's so beautiful. Did I really make it to heaven?'

To which St Peter replied, 'Yes, my dear, these are the gates to heaven. But you must do one more thing before you can enter.'

The woman was very excited, and asked St Peter what she must do to pass through the gates. 'Spell a word,' St Peter replied. 'What word?' she asked 'Any word,' answered St Peter. 'It's your choice.'

The woman promptly replied, 'Then the word I will spell is love. L-o-v-e.'

St Peter congratulated her on her good fortune to have made it to heaven, and asked her if she would mind taking his place at the gates for a few minutes while he went to the bathroom. 'I'd be honoured,' she said, 'but what should I do if someone comes while you are gone?'

St Peter reassured her, and instructed the woman simply to have any newcomers to the pearly gates to spell a word as she had done.

So the woman is left sitting in St Peter's chair and watching the beautiful angels soaring around her, when lo and behold, a man approaches the gates, and she realises it is her husband.

'What happened?' she cried. 'Why are you here?'

Her husband stared at her for a moment, then said, 'I was so upset when I left your funeral, I was in an accident. And now I am here? Did I really make it to heaven?' to which the woman replied, 'Not yet. You must spell a word first.'

'What word?' he asked. The woman responded, 'Czechoslovakia.'

There were three guys talking in the pub. Two of them were talking about the amount of control they have over their wives, while the third remained quiet.

After a while one of the first two turns to the third and says, 'Well, what about you, what sort of control do you have over your wife?'

The third fellow says, 'I'll tell you. Just the other night my wife came to me on her hands and knees.'

The first two guys were amazed. 'Wow! What happened then?' they asked.

The third man took a healthy swallow of his beer, sighed and muttered, 'She said, "Get out from under the bed and fight like a man."'

Tech Support Request

Last year I upgraded Girlfriend 1.0 to Wife 1.0 and noticed that the new program began unexpected child processing that took up a lot of space and valuable resources. No mention of this phenomenon was included in the product brochure. In addition, Wife 1.0 installs itself into all other programs and launches during system initialisation where it monitors all other system activity. Applications such as Pokernight 10.3 and Beerbash 2.5 no longer run, crashing the system whenever selected. I cannot seem to purge Wife1.0 from my system. I am thinking about going back to Girlfriend 1.0 but un-install does not work on this program. Can you help me?

Dear Sir —

This is a very common problem men complain about but is mostly due to a primary misconception. Many people upgrade from Girlfriend 1.0 to Wife 1.0 with the idea that Wife 1.0 is merely a 'UTILITIES and ENTERTAINMENT' program. Wife 1.0 is an OPERATING SYSTEM and designed by its creator to run everything. WARNING DO NOT TRY TO: un-install, delete or purge the program from the system once installed. Trying to un-install Wife1.0 can be disastrous. Doing so may destroy your hard and/or floppy drive. Trying to un-install or remove Wife 1.0 will destroy valuable system resources. You cannot go back to Girlfriend 1.0 because Wife 1.0 is not designed to do this. Some have tried to install Girlfriend 2.0 or Wife 2.0 but end up with more problems than the original system. Look in your manual under Warnings-Alimony/Child Support. Others have tried to run Girlfriend 1.0 in the background, while Wife 1.0 is running. Eventually Wife 1.0 detects Girlfriend 1.0 and a system conflict occurs, this can lead to a non-recoverable system crash. Some users have tried to download similar products such as Fling and 1NiteStand. Often their systems have become infected with a virus. I recommend you keep Wife 1.0 and just deal with the situation. Having Wife 1.0 installed myself, I might also suggest you read the entire section regarding General Protection Faults (GPFs). You must assume all responsibility for faults and problems that might occur. The best course of action will be to push apologise button then reset button as soon as lock-up occurs. System will run smooth as long as you take the blame for all GPFs. Wife 1.0 is a great program but is very high maintenance.

Suggestions for improved operation of Wife 1.0 — Monthly use utilities such as TLC and FTD.

Frequently use Communicator 5.0

Tech Support

The following is from an actual 1950s home economics book intended for secondary school girls, teaching them how to prepare for married life.

1. Have dinner ready. Plan ahead, even the night before, to have a delicious meal — on time. This is a way of letting him know that you have been thinking about him and are concerned about his needs. Most men are hungry when they come home and the prospects of a good meal are part of the warm welcome needed.

2. Prepare yourself. Take fifteen minutes to rest so you will be refreshed when he arrives. Touch up your make-up, put a ribbon in your hair and be fresh looking. He has just been with a lot of work-weary people. Be a little gay and a little more interesting. His boring day may need a lift.

3. Clear away clutter. Make one last trip through the main part of the house just before your husband arrives, gathering up school books, toys, paper, etc. Then run a dust cloth over the tables. Your husband will feel he has reached a haven of rest and order, and it will give you a lift too.

4. Prepare the children. Take a few minutes to wash the children's hands and faces if they are small, comb their hair, and if necessary, change their clothes. They are little treasures and he would like to see them playing the part.

5. Minimise the noise. At the time of his arrival, eliminate all noise of washer, dryer or vacuum. Try to encourage the children to be quiet. Greet him with a warm smile and be glad to see him.

6. Some DONT'S: Don't greet him with problems or complaints. Don't complain if he's late for dinner. Count this as minor compared with what he might have gone through that day.

7. Make him comfortable. Have him lean back in a comfortable chair or suggest he lies down in the bedroom. Have a cool or warm drink ready for him. Arrange his pillow and offer to take off his shoes. Speak in a low, soft, soothing and pleasant voice. Allow him to relax and unwind.

8. Listen to him. You may have a dozen things to tell him, but the moment of his arrival is not the time. Let him talk first.

9. Make the evening his. Never complain if he does not take you out to dinner or to other places of entertainment; instead try to understand his world of strain and pressure and his need to be home and relax.

10. The goal: try to make your home a place of peace and order where your husband can relax.

Martyrdom

The story of Columbine High School, Colorado.

In 1998, two boys with guns entered the school and killed thirteen children. Eight of them were committed Christians and were deliberately targeted by the murderers.

One of them was Cassie Bernell, a seventeen-year-old with long blonde hair. She had wanted to cut her hair to make wigs for cancer patients. She had become a Christian in 1996, radically converted after dabbling in the occult. She was described as a 'light for Christ' in the school and carried her Bible everywhere.

On the terrible day, she was reading the Bible in the school library. One of the killers pointed his gun at her and said,

'Do you believe in God?'

'Yes, I believe!' she replied.

'Why?'

The gunman shot her before she gave her answer.

Classmate Mickie Cain told Larry King on CNN, 'She completely stood up for God.'

The night she was murdered, Cassie's brother Chris found a poem she had written just two days before her death. In it was this line:

'Whatever it takes, I will be one who lives in the fresh newness of life of those who are alive from the dead.'

On 15th September 1999, a gunman entered Wedgwood Baptist Church (USA) and killed seven people and injured seven others before taking his own life. What God did after the shooting was not reported by the press. The Wedgewood Church office reported the following:

We have received over 10,000 e-mails, 5,000 cards, and $60,000 from all over the world. Al Meredith, our pastor, presented the gospel beautifully on *Larry King Live* when prompted by a question asked by Vice President Al Gore.

Because of the live news coverage and interviews, over 200 million people have heard the gospel because of this tragedy.

CNN also broadcast the memorial service live. Amazingly, because one of the victim's families lives and works in Saudi Arabia, that country allowed the service to be broadcast there as well. In Saudi Arabia it is illegal to say the name of Jesus on the street.

Because of that same CNN broadcast, thirty-five people in Japan gave their lives to Christ.

At several schools, students met around their flagpoles the next day. At one school twenty-five students accepted Christ, and one hundred and ten at another.

A teacher led twenty-two students to Christ in her classroom.

Christian teachers all over North Texas have been able to share with their classes because the students are asking questions about their teachers' faith.

On the east coast, where *See You at the Pole* was delayed because of the hurricane, record numbers of kids showed up to pray.

Governor Bush has visited our pastor several times. Just think of the influence our pastor could have if Governor Bush is the next president!

A caller to an area Christian radio station said that he didn't know what those people had but he wanted it. The DJ proceeded to lead him to Christ.

We have had over 70,000 hits on our web page which displays the plan of salvation in multiple languages.

Many members at Wedgwood Baptist are healing broken relationships within the body and experiencing spiritual renewal.

Every time the gunman fired a bullet, he intended to take a life. Yet God turned that around and saved several lives for each bullet fired. The faith of those who died has been multiplied many times over.

Men

Ten reasons why men should not become ordained ministers!

1. Men are too emotional to be vicars. Their conduct at football matches proves this.
2. A man's place is in the army not in the church.
3. Some men are so handsome that they'd distract women worshippers.
4. Their physical build indicates that men are more suited to tasks such as chopping down trees and wrestling mountain lions.
5. In the New Testament, the person who betrayed Jesus was a MAN.
6. Men are overly prone to violence. They settle disputes by fighting. Thus they would be dangerously unstable in a leadership role.
7. Man was created before woman, obviously as a prototype. Thus they represent an experiment rather than the crowning achievement of creation.
8. To be a vicar is to take on a nurturing role, which is traditionally the woman's role.
9. Men can still do church activities without being ordained, eg. clearing church paths, repairing the roof, maybe even leading the singing on Father's Day.
10. No woman in a congregation is going to respect a man who wears a skirt!

A man is walking along the beach and comes across an old bottle. He picks it up, pulls out the cork, and out pops a genie.

'Thank you for freeing me from the bottle,' says the genie, 'In return I shall grant you three wishes.'

'Great!' says the man. 'I always dreamed of this and I know exactly what I want. First, I want a billion pounds in a Swiss bank account.'

Poof! There in a flash of light was a piece of paper with account numbers on it.

'Second, I want a brand-new red Ferrari right now,' he continued.

Poof! There is a flash of light and a red Ferrari appears, right next to him.

'Thirdly, I want to be irresistible to women.'

Poof! There is a flash of light and he turns into a box of chocolates!

An English professor wrote the words, 'a woman without her man is nothing' on the blackboard, and directed the students to punctuate it correctly.

The men wrote: 'A woman, without her man, is nothing.'

The women wrote: 'A woman: without her, man is nothing.'

Punctuation is everything

Mum and Dad were watching TV when Mum said, 'I'm tired, and it's getting late. I think I'll go to bed.'

She went to the kitchen to make sandwiches for the next day's lunches, rinsed out the dessert bowls, took meat out of the freezer for supper the following evening, checked the cereal box levels, filled the sugar container, put spoons and bowls on the table and started the coffee pot for brewing the next morning. She then put some wet clothes in the dryer, put a load of clothes into the wash, ironed a shirt and sewed on a loose button. She picked up the game pieces left on the table and put the telephone book back into the drawer.

She watered the plants, emptied a wastepaper basket and hung up a towel to dry. She yawned and stretched and headed for the bedroom. She stopped by the desk and wrote a note to the teacher, counted out some cash for the school outing, and pulled a textbook out from under the chair.

She signed a birthday card for a friend, addressed and stamped the envelope and wrote a quick list for the supermarket. She put both near her purse.

Mum then creamed her face, put on moisturiser, brushed and flossed her teeth and trimmed her nails. Hubby called, 'I thought you were going to bed.'

'I'm on my way,' she said. She put some water into the dog's bowl and put the cat outside, then made sure the doors were locked. She looked in on each of the children and turned out a bedside lamp, hung up a shirt, threw some dirty socks in the laundry basket, and had a brief conversation with the one still up doing homework. In her own room, she set the alarm, laid out clothing for the next day, and straightened up the shoe rack. She added three things to her list of things to do for tomorrow.

About that time, the hubby turned off the TV and announced to no one in particular, 'I'm going to bed.' And he did.

Ministers

The results of a computerised survey of the traits of the perfect minister indicates the following characteristics:

Preaches for exactly twenty minutes and includes all the Bible has to say on the sermon subject.

Condemns everybody's sin except yours and never says anything anyone might disagree with.

Works from six am to midnight and gets eight hours sleep and stays healthy.

Is also the cleaner after each service.

Prepares sermons every week for forty years and never repeats an idea, an illustration or a joke.

Earns £100 a week, wears good clothes, buys good books, drives a new car and gives £50 a week from his own salary to the poor.

Is thirty-eight years old and has been in the ministry for twenty-five years.

Half of their hair is youthful and the other half is grey to give them that distinguished look.

Has a burning desire to work with teenagers and spends all of his time with senior citizens.

Is a close friend to every member.

Smiles all the time with a straight face because he has a sense of humour which keeps him seriously dedicated to his work.

Makes fifteen visits a day to church families, and visits all the sick every day.

Spends all of his time evangelising and is always in the office when you need him.

He has four children that never get in trouble and a wife who cooks cordon bleu like Delia Smith, has written books on prayer like Joyce Huggett and looks like Madonna without making anyone else jealous.

Misunderstanding

Linda Burnett, twenty-three, was visiting her in-laws, and while there went to a nearby supermarket to pick up some groceries. Several people noticed her sitting in her car with the windows rolled up and with her eyes closed, with both hands behind the back of her head.

One customer who had been at the store for a while became concerned and walked over to the car. He noticed that Linda's eyes were now open, and she looked very strange. He asked her if she was OK, and Linda replied that she'd been shot in the back of the head, and had been holding her brains in for over an hour.

The man called the paramedics, who broke into the car because the doors were locked and Linda refused to remove her hands from her head. When they finally got in, they found that Linda had a wad of bread dough on the back of her head. A Pillsbury biscuit canister had exploded from the heat, making a loud noise that sounded like a gunshot, and the wad of dough hit her in the back of her head. When she reached back to find out what it was, she felt the dough and thought it was her brains.

She initially passed out, but quickly recovered and tried to hold her brains in for over an hour until someone noticed and came to her aid.

Money

Money can buy medicine but it cannot buy health,
It can buy a house but not a home,
It can buy companionship but not friendship,
It can buy entertainment but not happiness,
It can buy food but not an appetite,
It can buy a bed but it cannot buy sleep,
It can buy a crucifix but not a Saviour,
It can buy a good life but not eternal life.

Morality

In 1997, a class of five to seven-year-olds constructed their own Ten Commandments for today's world:

1. You must not smash windows.
2. Don't steal things.
3. Don't kick and punch and bite and scratch.
4. Share with others.
5. Don't say rude things to God.
6. Have respect for others.
7. If someone's going up a mountain, don't pull their legs.
8. Don't hit people on the head with hammers.
9. Don't swear.
10. Don't pollute the land.

but I didn't hit him on the head with a hammer – I hit him on the toe. There's no commandment about that!

Mothers

A few months ago, when I was picking up the children at school, another mother I knew well rushed up to me. Emily was fuming with indignation.

'Do you know what you and I are?' she demanded. Before I could answer and I didn't really have one handy, she blurted out the reason for her question. It seemed she had just returned from renewing her driver's license at the County Clerk's office. Asked by the woman recorder to state her 'occupation', Emily had hesitated, uncertain how to classify herself.

'What I mean is,' explained the recorder, 'do you have a job, or are you just a...?'

'Of course I have a job,' snapped Emily. 'I'm a mother.'

'We don't list "mother" as an occupation..."housewife" covers it,' said the recorder emphatically.

I forgot all about her story until one day I found myself in the same situation, this time at our own Town Hall. The clerk was obviously a career woman, poised, efficient, and possessed of a high-sounding title, like 'Official Interrogator' or 'Town Registrar'.

'And what is your occupation?' she probed.

What made me say it, I do not know. The words simply popped out. 'I'm...a Research Associate in the field of Child Development and Human Relations.'

The clerk paused, ball-point pen frozen in midair, and looked up as though she had not heard right. I repeated the title slowly, emphasizing the most significant words. Then I stared with wonder as my pompous pronouncement was written in bold, black ink on the official questionnaire.

'Might I ask,' said the clerk

with new interest, 'just what you do in your field?'

Coolly, without any trace of fluster in my voice, I heard myself reply, 'I have a continuing program of research (what mother doesn't) in the laboratory and in the field (normally I would have said indoors and out). I'm working for my Masters (the whole darned family) and already have four credits (all daughters). Of course, the job is one of the most demanding in the humanities (any mother care to disagree?) and I often work fourteen hours a day (twenty-four is more like it). But the job is more challenging than most run-of-the-mill careers and the rewards are in satisfaction rather than just money.'

There was an increasing note of respect in the clerk's voice as she completed the form, stood up, and personally ushered me to the door. As I drove into our driveway buoyed up by my glamorous new career, I was greeted by my lab assistants — ages thirteen, seven, and three. And upstairs, I could hear our new experimental model (six months) in the child-development program, testing out a new vocal pattern.

I felt triumphant. I had scored a beat on bureaucracy. And I had gone down on the official records as someone more distinguished and indispensable to mankind than 'just another…'

Home…what a glorious career. Especially when there's a title on the door.

The ill-prepared student sat in his life science exam staring at a question on the final exam paper.

'Give four advantages of breast milk.'

What to write? He sighed, and began to scribble whatever came into his head, hoping for the best:

1. No need to boil.
2. Cats can't steal it.
3. Available whenever necessary.

So far so good. But the question demanded a fourth answer. Again, what to write? Once more, he sighed.

Suddenly, he took his pen and wrote his final answer:

4. Available in attractive containers.

One afternoon a man came home from work to find total mayhem in his house. His three children were outside, still in their pyjamas, playing in the mud, with empty food boxes and wrappers strewn all around the front yard. The door of his wife's car was open, as was the front door to the house. Proceeding inside, he found an even bigger mess. A lamp had been knocked over, and the rug was wadded against one wall. In the front room the TV was loudly blaring, and the family room was strewn with toys and various items of clothing. In the kitchen, dishes filled the sink, breakfast food was spilled on the counter, dog food was spilled on the floor, a broken glass lay under the table, and a small pile of sand was spread by the back door.

He quickly headed up the stairs, stepping over toys and more piles of clothes, looking for his wife. He was worried she might be ill, or that something serious had happened. He found her lounging in the bedroom, still curled in the bed in her pyjamas, reading a novel. She looked up at him, smiled, and asked how his day went.

He looked at her in bewilderment and asked, 'What happened here today?'

She again smiled and answered, 'You know every day when you come home from work you ask me what in the world I did all day?'

'Yes,' was his incredulous reply.

She answered, 'Well, today I didn't do it.'

Now I lay me down to sleep,
I pray my sanity to keep.
For if some peace I do not find,
I'm pretty sure I'll lose my mind.

I pray I find a little quiet
Far from the daily family riot
May I lie back — not have to think
about what they're stuffing down
　　the sink,
or who they're with, or where
　　they're at
and what they're doing to the cat.

I pray for time all to myself
(did something just fall off a shelf?)

To cuddle in my nice, soft bed
(Oh no, another goldfish — dead!)

Some silent moments for goodness
　　sake
(Did I just hear a window break?)
And that I need not cook or clean —
(well heck, I've got the right to
　　dream)

Yes now I lay me down to sleep,
I pray my wits about me keep,
But as I look around I know —
I must have lost them long ago!
Anon.

Motoring

The Christian Road Safety Association have come up with the following Ten Commandments for motoring:

1. Begin with a prayer
2. If you start late, arrive late
3. Alcohol is for the radiator, not for the operator
4. If entry into the flow of traffic is facilitated by the courtesy of another driver, wave in appreciation
5. If you have inadvertently endangered the safe passage of another vehicle, wave as an apology
6. Make it easy for aggressive opportunity snatchers to get ahead of you — far ahead
7. So drive that the sudden appearance of a patrol car is a pleasant sight
8. Give plenty of space to cars marked with dents
9. Never accelerate, and decelerate if advisable, when another car wishes to enter your lane
10. End every trip with a prayer of thanksgiving

N

Negativity

A magician was working on a cruise ship in the Caribbean. The audience would be different each week, so the magician allowed himself to do the same tricks over and over again.

There was only one problem — the captain's parrot saw the shows each week and began to understand how the magician did every trick. Once he understood he started shouting in the middle of the show, 'Look, it's not the same hat.'

'Look, he is hiding the flowers under the table.'

'Hey, why are all the cards the Ace of Spades?'

The magician was furious but couldn't do anything. After all, it *was* the captain's parrot. One stormy day the ship had an accident and sank. The magician found himself adrift on a piece of wood in the middle of the ocean… of course, the parrot was adrift on this very same piece of wood with him.

They stared at each other with hate, but did not utter a word. This went on for a day, then another, and then another. After almost three days the parrot finally says, 'OK, I give up. Where the heck is the boat?'

A farmer lived on the same farm all his life. It was a good farm, but with the passing years, the farmer began to tire a bit and he longed for a change, for something better.

Every day he found a new reason for criticising some feature of the farm. Finally, he decided to sell and contacted an agent, who promptly prepared a sale advertisement. As one might expect, it emphasised all the farm's advantages — ideal location, modern equipment, healthy stock, acres of fertile ground, etc. Before advertising, the agent called the farmer and read the copy to him for his approval. When he'd finished, the farmer said, 'Hold everything! I've changed my mind. I'm not going to sell. I've been looking for a place like that all my life!'

There was a man, approaching middle age, whose life was comfortable, but he felt an emptiness inside, a longing. So he decided to join a monastery.

The head monk told him that the road ahead was difficult, he would have to give up all earthly possessions, pray constantly, and he would have to be totally silent. In fact, he could not speak at all, to anyone. He was allowed only to say two words every five years.

So the man joins and becomes a monk, and he is silent.

Five years goes by, and the Pope comes to visit. The man is summoned before the Pope, and he is asked, 'So, how is everything?' The man answers 'Bed hard'. The Pope replies, 'Oh, I'm so sorry, we didn't know. We'll take care of that right away. You should be comfortable in bed.' And the bed is fixed.

Another five years goes by, the man is silent, and again, the Pope comes to visit. He again asks, 'How are you, my son, is all OK?' The man replies to the Pope, 'Food cold', to which the Pope replies, 'Oh my, that is no good, we will take care of that problem right away. No more cold food.'

Again, five more years goes by, the man is the ideal monk, he prays, he is silent. This time, the Pope can't visit, so the man is called before his superior, who asks, 'How are you, are you OK? To which the man replies, 'I quit.'

So his superior says, in surprise, 'Well, of course you quit, you've been here for fifteen years and all you've done is complain!'

Negligence

South African Health — Pelonomi Hospital (26 May 1996, 10:08).

'For several months our nurses have been baffled to find a dead patient in the same bed every Friday morning' a spokeswoman for the Pelonomi Hospital (Free State, South Africa) told reporters. 'There was no apparent cause for any of the deaths, and extensive checks on the air conditioning system, and a search for possible bacterial infection, failed to reveal any clues. However, further inquiries have now revealed the cause of these deaths. It seems that every Friday morning a cleaner would enter the ward, remove the plug that powered the patient's life-support system, plug her floor polisher into the vacant socket, then go about her business. When she had finished her chores, she would plug the life-support machine back in and leave, unaware that the patient was now dead. She could not, after all, hear the screams and eventual death rattle over the whirring of her polisher. We are sorry, and have sent a strong letter to the cleaner in question. Further, the Free State Health and Welfare Department is arranging for an electrician to fit an extra socket, so there should be no repetition of this incident. The enquiry is now closed.'

From *Cape Times*, 6/13/96. The headline of the newspaper story was, 'Cleaner Polishes Off Patients'.

Nervousness

The new priest was so nervous at his first mass that he could hardly speak. Before his second appearance in the pulpit, he asked the Monsignor how he could relax.

The Monsignor said, 'Next Sunday, it may help if you put some vodka in the water pitcher. After a few sips everything should go smoothly.'

The next Sunday the new priest put the suggestion into practice and was able to talk up a storm. He felt great! However, upon returning to the presbytery he found a note from the Monsignor:

Dear Father
1. Next time sip rather than gulp.
2. There are ten commandments, not twelve.
3. There are twelve disciples, not ten.
4. We do not refer to the cross as the 'Big T'.
5. The recommended grace before meals is not 'Rub-a-dub-dub, thanks for the grub. Yeah God!'

Newspapers

Actual excerpts from classified sections of city newspapers:

Illiterate? Write today for free help.

Dog for sale: eats anything and is fond of children.

Man wanted to work in dynamite factory. Must be willing to travel.

Three-year-old teacher needed for pre-school. Experience preferred.

Mixing bowl set designed to please a cook with round bottom for efficient beating.

For sale: antique desk suitable for lady with thick legs and large drawers.

We do not tear your clothing with machinery. We do it carefully by hand.

Used cars: Why go elsewhere to be cheated. Come here first.

Our bikinis are exciting. They are simply the tops.

Wanted. Widower with school-age children requires person to assume general housekeeping duties. Must be capable of contributing to growth of family.

Notices

A preacher went to speak at a church. He was due to speak at both the morning and the evening services on the Sunday. In the morning he took as his text the parable of the wise and foolish virgins. In the evening he chose to give a call to the mission field.

The local church, seeking to draw attention to the visit, produced a big poster advertising the coming Sunday meetings and put it on their notice-board. They combined the titles of the two messages without realising the effect of their combination.

The top of the poster read: 'FIVE VIRGINS IN A CRISIS.'

The bottom read: 'WHAT CAN ONE MAN DO?'

O

Obedience

Never have anything
'your way';
have everything
'Yahweh'.

'No man ever got
lost on a straight
road.'
Abraham Lincoln

Jesus was one
child who knew
more than his
parents, yet he
obeyed them.

Overwork

For a couple of years I've been blaming it on lack of sleep and too much pressure from my job, but now I've found out the real reason:

I am tired because I am overworked.

The population of this country is 58 million.

24 million are retired.

That leaves 34 million to do the work.

There are 20 million at school, which leaves 14 million to do the work.

Of this there are 7.5 million employed by the government, leaving 6.5 million to do the work.

2.7 million are in the armed forces, which leaves 3.8 million to do the work.

Take from the total the 3,770,000 people who work for local authorities and that leaves 30,000 to do the work.

At any given time there are 20,000 people in hospital, leaving 10,000 to do the work.

Now there are 9,998 people in prison.

That leaves just two people to do the work.

You and me.

And you're sitting here reading jokes.

P

Parents

'Before I was married I had three theories about raising children. Now I have three children and no theories.' **John Wilmot**, Earl of Rochester (1647-1680)

Percentage of fathers who say they read to their kids: 61
Percentage of kids who agree with this figure: 28

How to make a child into a delinquent: Ten easy rules from the police department, Houston, Texas.

1. Begin at infancy to give the child everything he wants. In this way he will grow up to believe the world owes him a living.
2. When she picks up bad language, laugh at her. This will make her think she's cute.
3. Never give him any spiritual training. Wait until he's twenty-one, and then let him 'decide for himself'.
4. Avoid the use of the word 'wrong'. It may develop a guilt complex.
5. Pick up everything she leaves lying around — books, shoes, clothes. Do everything for her so that she will be experienced in throwing all responsibility on others.
6. Let him read any printed matter he can get his hands on. Be careful that the silverware and glasses are sterilised, but let his mind feast on rubbish.
7. Quarrel frequently in the presence of your children. In this way they will not be too shocked when the home is broken up.
8. Give a child all the spending money she wants. Never let her earn her own. Why should she have things as tough as you had them?
9. Satisfy his craving for food and drink and comfort. See that every sensual desire is gratified. Denial may lead to harmful frustration.
10. Take her part against neighbours, teachers, policemen. They are prejudiced against your child.

Here are ten simple activities for expectant parents to help prepare them before the arrival of their first child:

1. Women, put on a dressing gown, stick a bean-bag down your front, leave it there for nine months. After nine months, take out only 10% of the beans.

2. Before you have your baby, find a couple who have just had one. Criticise them for their lack of discipline, patience, tolerance, wisdom, etc. Enjoy the moment to the full — it'll be the last time you will have all the answers.

3. Walk around the sitting room from 5-10pm carrying a wet bag weighing about 10lbs. At 10pm put it down, set the alarm for midnight, and fall asleep. Get up then and walk with the wet bag till 1am. Then set the alarm for 3am. Repeat procedure till the morning. Keep this up for five years and look cheerful.

4. Smear peanut butter over your sofa and jam on the curtains. Hide a fish finger behind the TV and leave it there all summer.

5. To practise dressing a child, buy an octopus and a string bag. Try putting the octopus in the string bag without any of its arms hanging out. Time allowed for this activity — all morning.

6. Take an egg carton. Using scissors and paint, turn it into an alligator. Now take a toilet tube. Using only sellotape and a piece of foil, turn it into a Christmas cracker. Finally, take a milk container, a table-tennis ball, and an empty packet of Coco Pops and make an exact model of the Eiffel Tower.

7. Get rid of your sports car and buy a Volvo estate. Then buy a chocolate ice-cream and put it in the glove compartment. Get a coin and stick it in the cassette player. Take a family-size packet of Kit-Kats and mash them all over the back seats. Finally, run a garden rake along both sides of the car.

8. Always repeat everything you say at least five times.

9. Go to the local supermarket with a fully grown goat (the nearest equivalent to a small child). Buy the week's groceries without letting the goat out of your sight and without the goat eating anything or making a mess.

10. Hollow out a melon. Make a small, mouth-sized hole in the side. Hang it from the ceiling of your kitchen and swing it from side to side. Now get a bowl of soggy Weetabix and attempt to spoon it into the swinging melon by pretending to be an aeroplane. Continue until half the Weetabix is gone. Tip the rest into your lap, making sure that a lot of it falls on the floor.

Anon.

Whenever your kids are out of control, you can take comfort from the thought that even God's omnipotence did not extend to God's kids.

After creating heaven and earth, God created Adam and Eve. And the first thing he said was:

'Don't.'

'Don't what?' Adam replied.

'Don't eat the forbidden fruit.' God said.

'Forbidden fruit? We've got forbidden fruit? Hey, Eve...we've got forbidden fruit!'

'No way!'

'Yes!'

'Don't eat that fruit!' said God.

'Why?'

'Because I am your Father and I said so!' said God, wondering why he hadn't stopped after making the elephants.

A few minutes later God saw his children having an apple break and was angry.

'Didn't I tell you not to eat the fruit?' the First Parent asked.

'Uh huh,' Adam replied.

'Then why did you?'

'I dunno,' Eve answered.

'She started it!' Adam said.

'Did not!'

'Did too!'

'DID NOT!'

Having had it with the two of them, God's punishment was that Adam and Eve should have children of their own. Thus, the pattern was set and it has never changed.

But there is reassurance in this story. If you have persistently and lovingly tried to give them wisdom and they haven't taken it, don't be hard on yourself. If God had trouble handling children, what makes you think it would be a piece of cake for you?

Advice for the day: If you have a lot of tension and you get a headache, do what it says on the aspirin bottle: take two and keep away from children.

It all started so innocently. Here I was, doing God's work. I was happy. I wasn't looking for an affair. But it happens to pastors, and the results can be devastating.

I saw a real need. My pastor's heart responded to her needs. My efforts on her behalf were met with warmth, understanding and acceptance. I felt needed. I saw in her eyes sparks of excitement for my godly attention, and it felt good. It was innocent and well meaning, not intended to foster an affair.

It was good to be appreciated. The bottom line was that she made me feel important. No, I did not want to be unfaithful to my wife. True, our marriage wasn't as exciting as it had been earlier. My wife and I had got involved in different interests and activities. Our days schedules were so full that we hardly saw each other, and when we did we were both so tired that it was just flat — no excitement.

But with her it was different — electric, powerful, energising.

Then there were the children. My own children were doing well in school, with two loving parents providing for all their needs. Her children? Little support, massive needs, lots of hurting. After all, my children have a mother, even if I'm not there.

Slowly, the 'friend' became a mistress. There were the extra hours of counselling that couldn't wait. There were more and more 'evening appointments' that took me away from home. I could sense my wife's anxiety and puzzlement, but I kept spending time with 'her'. My spouse kept quiet about what was going on, but I could detect a smouldering resentment that drove us even further apart, and made my contacts with 'her' even more desirable to me. It was easy to rationalise that if my wife were more attuned to my needs, I might spend more time at home.

Soon I noticed a subtle shift in my own attitude. At home I was husband and dad. That's fine, I guess. But with her I was a hero! She appreciated everything I did, and looked at me with loving, longing, unquestioning eyes. I enjoyed spending time with her. She fed my ego and I craved more of her delicacies.

One day she called me and gave an open invitation: 'I know it may be hard for you, but I want you for a whole weekend. It's a little place up in the mountains, and honestly, I need you. No one else will do. Please say yes!' Her voice was plaintive and sincere. Heady stuff this. When did my spouse last make such a clear invitation and show that same eagerness to have me with her?

I knew I should have said no, but there was a part of me that needed the recognition. Part of me wanted to be wanted. Besides, the Bible says we are to comfort the widow, the lonely, the needy, the hurting. My own family is well cared for. They don't need that much of my attention. And here's one who craves my presence, can't get along without me.

I said yes. Not once, but again, and again and again. I was hooked into a full-blown affair. I loved my mistress, and she returned that love to me.

My family was not cut off. Just there. We had no animosity at home, just less and less involvement. My wife and I went from being lovers to being room-mates.

My mistress and I had lots of exciting experiences together: picnics, long evenings of discussion, talk of the future for both of us. We even prayed together. In fact, we prayed together lots. That is one of the things that made the affair seem so right, so positive, so acceptable. Our intimacies increased to the point where I felt responsible for her every need, and she called me for every major decision. Our lives seemed to blend together in a warm bond of loving trust and mutual joy.

Then a cold splash of reality hit me like a bucket of ice water. She's not my bride, and never will be. She informed me that she belongs to someone else. I had to make some tough decisions. Caught between needing and wanting her attention and affection, and drawing on my own somewhat neglected marriage for those needs to be met, I felt like a fool.

I felt so vulnerable, so ashamed. So scared of admitting what had gone on. What would I tell my wife and my own children? How about, 'Oh, hi there, family — I'm back. Sorry to have had an affair. Hope it didn't hurt you too much?' Or 'Well, to tell the truth, I just got caught up with my own ego needs and began to invest in the affair until there was nothing left for the family.' Or could my wife understand how the involvement had moved her out of my affection focus, yet I still loved her as my wife? Could I manage to overcome the affair and still have a marriage and family?

I didn't want it to be this way. It began with sincere devotion and paying attention to her needs (strange — it started with her needing me, and changed to me needing her). Then my love and affection began to produce results in her. It fed my ego. It seemed so right, it felt so good! We were both so happy. But she began to pull me away from my own family responsibilities. I began to realise that sometimes I'd rather be with her than with my own wife and children. That's when I began to see the danger.

The affair, I sensed, could destroy everything. It is the affair pastors don't want to face or talk about — the affair with their church.

Anon.

Adolescence is when children start bringing up the parents.

The only thing that children wear out faster than shoes is parents and teachers.

'Children aren't fooled. They know we give time to the things we love.'
John Bradshaw

'Insanity is hereditary; you catch it from your children.'
J. John

Patience

Patience is a bitter plant that produces sweet fruit.

An apocryphal story emerged during World War Two about a meeting between Hitler, Mussolini and Churchill in 1940. They met for tea in Paris by a famous pond full of carp. Hitler claimed that he had won the war and was backed up by Mussolini. Churchill defied him. Realising that the meeting wouldn't progress very far, Churchill decided to resort to a wager. He suggested that the first person to catch a carp without using fishing equipment would be the winner of the war.

Hitler pulled out his revolver and shot at the fish but missed.

Mussolini jumped in and tried with his bare hands, but failed.

Churchill got out a spoon and started tossing water over his shoulder.

When asked why, he replied, 'It will take a long time, but we're going to win!'

Persecution

More Christians died for their faith in the twentieth century than in the previous nineteen centuries combined. More than 160,000 were martyred in 1996 because of their belief in Jesus. Countless others were raped, beaten, tortured and were subjected to unimaginable horrors. Persecution appears to be escalating exponentially.

A Jewish journalist called Michael Horowitz is presently championing the cause of the suffering church. He wrote:

Christians have become the targets of the thug regimes around the world, and they are many. What's going on now is monumental, and it's affecting millions, tens of millions, of people. We're not talking about discrimination, but persecution of the worst sort: slavery, starvation, murder, looting, burning, torture.

400 believers will die for their faith today.

Perseverance

> **Saints are sinners who kept on trying.**

The way to get to the top is to get off your bottom.

In the 1880s, some of the world's finest engineers were assembled to give their advice about building a railway through the Andes mountains. All of them bar one said the job couldn't be done, a Polish engineer called Ernest Malinowski. He was sixty years old.

Malinowski assured the advisors that he was the man for the job and got on with it. The railway line was eventually built and finished. It went through 62 tunnels and across 30 bridges. One tunnel was 4,000 feet long and 15,000 feet above sea level. The work was held up twice by revolutions. On one occasion, Malinowski had to escape the country to Peru. In the end, he hurdled *every* obstacle.

When things go wrong, as they sometimes will
When the road you're trudging seems all up hill
When the funds are low, and the debts are high
And you want to smile, but you have to sigh
When care is pressing you down a bit
Rest if you must, but don't you quit.

Success is failure turned inside out
The silver tint of clouds of doubt
And you never can tell how close you are
It may be near when it seems so far
So stick to the fight when you're hardest hit
It's when things seem worse
That you must not quit.

Anon.

The film *Chariots Of Fire* received an Oscar as best film in 1981. At first glance, it seemed improbable that a film based on this story would have achieved such popularity and such acclaim, for the film is simply the story of Eric Liddell, a man who would not run an Olympic race on Sunday.

In 1924 Eric Liddell had a preliminary draw on a Sunday. He refused to run, casting doubt about his loyalty to his king and country and about the balance of his mind. He was subsequently moved from the 100 metres race to the 400 metres. Just before he ran the race someone gave him a piece of paper with a Bible text:'Those who honour me I will honour' (1 Samuel 2:30).

He ran. He won and broke the world record for the 400 metres.

Trying times are not the times to stop trying.

Rule 1 — take one more step.
Rule 2 — when you don't think you can take one more step, refer to rule 1.

The world has a lot of starters but very few finishers.

Perseverance is not a long race, it is many short races one after another.

To the end

Smith Wigglesworth, just after preaching his last sermon, went to heaven in the vestry of the church. The following rare letter was found in Smith's pocket addressed to his good friend Mrs Helen Reid, wife of Pastor Andrew Reid of Scotland. Helen had been saved under the ministry of Evan Roberts when she visited Wales from Scotland. Smith had also prayed for her son James who was healed of cancer of the brain. Andrew and Smith were the closest of friends.

From 70, Victor Road,
Heaton, Bradford, Yorks.

March 11, 1947

My dear Sister in Jesus!
    Many thanks for your letter received.
    All saints are being tried. This is a proof that we are his, but we are more than conquerors through him. The trial of your faith is more precious than gold tried in the fire.
    On January 4th this year God gave me a real victory over a bad case of cancer. Early in the morning God gave me Luke 10:19, 'I will give you power over all the power of the enemy and nothing shall by any way hurt you.' (I prayed for) a very helpless case. Lost almost all flesh all strength (skin and bones, and without strength). She could not walk nor use her arms. The Lord's presence was so real. He himself wrought a great miracle as soon as hands were put upon her she was able to walk and use her arms and no more pain. About ten people came into the room and with one voice said, 'We have never seen anything like this before.'
    You can understand what joy and presence of God filled the house. So you can just imagine what the house was like full of joy in the Holy Ghost.
    Smith Wigglesworth.

Persistence

'The sense of obligation to continue is present in all of us. A duty to strive is the duty of us all. I felt a call to that duty.'
Abraham Lincoln

Probably the greatest example of persistence is Abraham Lincoln. If you want to learn about somebody who didn't quit, look no further.

Born into poverty, Lincoln was faced with defeat throughout his life. He lost eight elections, twice failed in business and suffered a nervous breakdown.

He could have quit many times — but he didn't and because he didn't quit, he became one of the greatest presidents in the history of the Untied States of America.

Lincoln was a champion and he never gave up. Here is a sketch of Lincoln's road to the White House:

1816   His family was forced out of their home. He had to work to support them.
1818   His mother died.
1831   Failed in business.
1832   Ran for state legislature — *lost.*
1832   Also lost his job — wanted to go to law school but couldn't get in.
1833   Borrowed some money from a friend to begin a business and by the end of the year he was bankrupt. He spent the next seventeen years of his life paying off this debt.
1834   Ran for state legislature again — *won.*
1835   Was engaged to be married, sweetheart died and his heart was broken.
1836   Had a nervous breakdown and was in bed for six months.
1838   Sought to become speaker of the state legislature — *defeated.*
1840   Sought to become elector — *defeated.*
1843   Ran for congress — lost.
1846   Ran for congress again — this time he won — went to Washington and did a good job.
1848   Ran for re-election to Congress — *lost.*
1849   Sought the job of land officer in his home state — *rejected.*
1854   Ran for Senate of the United States — lost.
1856   Sought the Vice-Presidential nomination at his party's national convention — got less than 100 votes.
1858   Ran for US Senate again — *again he lost.*
1860   *Elected President of the United States.*

'The path was worn and slippery, my foot slipped from under me, knocking the other out of the way, but I recovered and said to myself, "It's a slip and not a fall."'
Abraham Lincoln, after losing a senate race.

Did you know that when Charles Darrow brought the first prototype of the board game called Monopoly to Parker Brothers in 1934 they laughed him out of their offices?

They said, 'That is really a stupid game. It's never going to sell, it's far too complicated. It takes far too long to play. We are experts on games and we figure there are fifty-two major flaws in this game of Monopoly.'

But that didn't deter Charles Darrow; he began to market the game on his own. Within one year department stores sold 5,000 sets. It was such a hit that Parker Brothers confessed, 'Well maybe we were a little too hasty.' So they signed a contract with Charles Darrow, who became a multi-millionaire. They have since sold over 100 million sets of Monopoly in fifty-four countries and in twenty-six languages.

Parker Brothers have produced 3.2 billion of the little green houses.

If you were to take these little green houses and line them up, end to end, they would encircle the globe.

heh heh - did we? I can hardly remember...

My goodness! Another whopping royalties cheque! We must've sold millions by now – and to think you all said we wouldn't sell a single copy!

PARKER BROTHERS AND CO.

Thomas Gray wrote seventy-five drafts of his 'Elegy Written in a Country Churchyard' before he was satisfied with it.

Somerset Maugham earned only £250 in his first ten years as a writer.

George Gershwin composed almost a hundred tunes before he sold his first one — for $5.

It takes the hammer of persistence to drive the nail of success.

Perspective

If you have food in the refrigerator, clothes on your back, a roof overhead and a place to sleep, you are richer than 75% of this world.

If you have money in the bank, in your wallet, and spare change in a dish somewhere, you are among the top 8% of the world's wealthy.

If you woke up this morning with more health than illness, you are more blessed than the million who will not survive this week.

If you have never experienced the danger of battle, the loneliness of imprisonment, the agony of torture, or the pangs of starvation, you are ahead of 500 million people in the world.

If you can attend a church meeting without fear of harassment, arrest, torture or death, you are more blessed than three billion people in the world.

If you hold up your head with a smile on your face and are truly thankful, you are blessed because the majority can, but most do not.

If you can hold someone's hand, hug them or even touch them on the shoulder, you are blessed because you can offer healing touch.

If you can read this message, you are more blessed than over two billion people in the world who cannot read at all.

Should you find it hard to get to sleep tonight, just remember the homeless family who has no bed to lie in.

Should you find yourself stuck in traffic, don't despair; there are people in this world for whom driving is an unheard-of privilege.

Should you have a bad day at work, think of the man who has been out of work for the last three months.

Should you despair over a relationship gone wrong, think of the person who has never known what it's like to love and be loved in return.

Should you grieve the passing of another weekend, think of the woman in dire straits, working twelve hours a day, seven days a week, for £10 to feed her family.

Should your car break down, leaving you miles away from assistance, think of the paraplegic who would love the opportunity to take that walk.

Should you notice a new grey hair in the mirror, think of the cancer patient in chemotherapy who wishes she had hair to examine.

Should you find yourself at a loss and pondering what life is all about, asking, 'What is my purpose?' Be thankful: there are those who didn't live long enough to get the opportunity.

Should you find yourself the victim of other people's bitterness, ignorance, smallness or insecurities; remember, things could be worse. You could be them!

A letter from a girl in her first year of college who was desperately trying to gain sympathy and to give a new perspective on things.

Dear Mum and Dad

Since I left for college I have been remiss in writing and I am sorry for my thoughtlessness in not having written before.

I'll bring you up to date now but before you read on, please sit down. Are you sitting down? Don't read on unless you are....

I am getting along pretty well now, the skull fracture and concussion that I got when I jumped out of my dormitory window when it caught on fire shortly after my arrival here has pretty well healed. I only get those sick headaches once a day.

Fortunately the fire in my dorm and the jump was witnessed by an attendant at the petrol station. He ran over, took me to hospital and continued to visit me there. When I got out of the hospital I had nowhere to live because of the burnt-out conditions of my room so he was kind enough to invite me to share his basement bedroom flat with him. It's sort of small, but cute.

He is a very fine boy and we have fallen deeply in love and are planning to get married. We haven't set the exact date yet but it will be before my pregnancy begins to show. Yes, Mum and Dad, I'm pregnant! I know how much you are looking forward to being grandparents and I know you will welcome the baby and give it the same tender care and devotion that you gave me when I was a child.

The reason for the delay in our marriage is that my boyfriend has a minor infection which I carelessly caught from him. I know, however, that you will welcome him into our family with open arms. He is kind and although not well educated, he is ambitious. Although he is of a different race and religion than ours, I know that your often expressed tolerance will not permit you to be bothered by that.

In conclusion, now that I have brought you up to date, I want to tell you that there was no dormitory fire. I did not have concussion or skull fracture. I was not in the hospital, am not pregnant, I am not infected and there is no boyfriend in my life.

However, I am failing history and science and I wanted you to see these marks in their proper perspective!

Politics

The following speech was given by President Yoweri Museveni of Uganda at a 1998 regional meeting of African presidents held in Kampala.

Thank you, Your Excellencies, for the opportunity to share some thoughts about the spiritual condition of the peoples of Africa. As I observe the tribal differences, religious divisions, poverty and disease, lack of sufficient educational opportunities for our children, political upheaval and racial strife, it becomes obvious that the principles of Jesus Christ have not penetrated Africa enough!

It may seem strange for some of you to think that I would say this about Christ, because I know many of you may think this is too religious and not a very practical solution to the problems I have just mentioned. Furthermore, I know that most of you do not think of me as a very religious man — in fact, I do not think that about myself. My wife is a much better believer and pray-er than I am, and those who have known me through the years know that I have had problems with religious people. As I have grown older, I realise that all of the problems have not been theirs, but I do think that those of us who claim to love God ought to love one another — this is one of the most basic attributes of a follower of Christ.

As the years have gone by, however, even though I have not become a member of any special religious group, I have decided to follow Jesus Christ with my whole heart. I find in him the inner strength, the precepts and the lifestyle that can help me and all the people of Uganda to solve the problems we face individually and as a nation.

It is one of the interesting facts about Jesus Christ that people in every nation of the world regardless of religion, whether one is a believer or a non-believer, consider Jesus the greatest authority on human relations in history. His views on that subject have transcended all religions and cultures. It is remarkable that the person of Jesus Christ is accepted by everyone — even when they are not attracted by institutional religion.

With that in mind, I want to stress at least three significant precepts that Christ taught and modelled, which if practised, will help Africa: forgiveness, humility and love.

Forgiveness — Jesus Christ is the only person ever to come up with the idea of unconditional forgiveness, even of one's enemies. He went so far as to say, if you don't forgive, God won't forgive you. In countries where animosity and division go back for generations and even thousands of years, how can peace come to a person, a group of persons or a nation if at some point we do not forgive and let God take the vengeance on our enemies if that is what he decides to do? It has also been discovered that if we do not forgive, in the final analysis, it hurts us more to hate than it does those we hate. Therefore, I have come to the conclusion that the message of Christ on forgiveness is the only practical solution to healing a nation's wounds and bringing unity.

Humility — this is one of the most important attributes necessary to become a good leader. When you observe leaders at all levels of society, throughout Africa and I suppose throughout the world, you find them being overcome by power, greed and self-interest. Somehow, after they have attained the prominence and positions of trust, they forget the people, their poverty and need. They forget that they could become a great instrument to help their country, and instead they begin to live like little kings and dictators.

Only with a humble spirit, one which recognises that we who have been given opportunities greater than most are in fact servants of God and the people rather than masters, will we be able to help our countries move from Third World status and lead the people to a new day. As the Scripture says, God resists the proud and gives help to the humble. If you have time to pray for me, please pray that God will give me the strength, wisdom and sense to be a humble servant....

Love — it has been fascinating to me to discover that for centuries people who have been the most thoughtful, the most respected, and who have made the most lasting contributions to the human race have all agreed that the highest and greatest purpose for their lives has been to seek to love God with all their heart, mind, soul and strength. These are people like Moses — the great lawgiver; Abraham — the man of faith and father of nations; William Wilberforce — the leader against the slave trade; Mother Teresa, and on and on. Jesus Christ said the sum of all the law and prophets is to love God and love one another.

If love for God and one another were the rule and the prevailing attitude in our nations and communities, all problems would move gradually to resolution. Even when love is not the rule for most of the population and only exists among the few, great things happen that give hope and life in a world starved of love and caring.

Today, as we meet together, let's resolve to take Jesus Christ out of the religious setting in which we have imprisoned him and walk with him along the dusty roads of Africa where he feels much more at home.

> '**Politicians campaign in poetry
> but govern in prose.**'
> **Mario Cuomo**

Positive outlook

There were two ways David could have looked at Goliath. He could have said, 'Boy, he's so big, I'm out of here.' Or, he could have said, 'Boy, he's so big, I can't miss.' David did the latter.

'Instead of seeing the soldier on duty next to him as a galling restriction to the gospel, Paul saw him as a captive audience.' **Chuck Swindoll**

For all the negative things we have to say to ourselves, God has positive answers.

You say: It's impossible.
God says: All things are possible
(Luke 18:27).
You say: I'm too tired.
God says: I will give you rest
(Matthew 11:28-30).
You say: Nobody really loves me.
God says: I love you
(John 3:16; 13:34).
You say: I can't go on.
God says: My grace is sufficient
(2 Corinthians 12:9;
Psalm 91:15).
You say: I can't figure things out.
God says: I will direct your steps
(Proverbs 3:5-6).
You say: I can't do it.
God says: You can do all things
(Philippians 4:13).
You say: I'm not able.
God says: I am able
(2 Corinthians 9:8).
You say: It's not worth it.
God says: It will be worth it
(Roman 8:28).

You say: I can't forgive myself.
God says: I FORGIVE YOU
(1 John 1:9; Romans 8:1).
You say: I can't manage.
God says: I will supply all your needs
(Philippians 4:19).
You say: I'm afraid.
God says: I have not given you a
spirit of fear
(2 Timothy 1:7).
You say: I'm always worried and
frustrated.
God says: Cast all your cares on me
(1 Peter 5:7).
You say: I don't have enough faith.
God says: I've given everyone a
measure of faith
(Romans 12:3).
You say: I'm not clever enough.
God says: I give you wisdom
(1 Corinthians 1:30).
You say: I feel all alone.
God says: I will never leave you or
forsake you
(Hebrews 13:5).

Positive thinking

 I was going to buy a copy of *The Power of Positive Thinking*, and then I thought: What good would that do?

Prayer

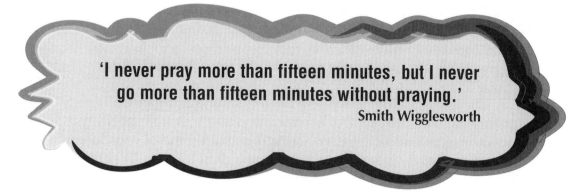

'I never pray more than fifteen minutes, but I never go more than fifteen minutes without praying.'

Smith Wigglesworth

'If a matter is not serious enough to pray about, then it is not serious enough to worry about; and if it is serious enough to pray about, and we have prayed about it, then there is no need to worry about it.'

James E. Gibbons

From the *Evening Standard*, 23 November 1999:

Heart attack patients who are prayed for appear to recover faster than those who aren't. At the Mid America Heart Institute in Kansas City, 500 patients admitted with heart attacks were allotted people to secretly pray for them, a further 500 were used as a control. Those in the prayer group had a significantly better recovery, being 11 per cent better off in terms of symptoms and test results. Patients and staff knew nothing about the trial, ruling out any placebo effect. Not exactly proof of the existence of God, but it could be evidence of some kind of subtle force of human consciousness. The researchers suggest thinking hard about someone in hospital with an attitude of prayer appears to be helpful.

As you got up this morning, I watched you and hoped you would talk to me, even if it was just a few words, asking my opinion or thanking me for something good that happened in your life yesterday — but I noticed you were too busy trying to find the right outfit to put on and wear to work.

I waited again. When you ran around the house getting ready I knew there would be a few minutes for you to stop and say hello, but you were too busy. At one point you had to wait fifteen minutes with nothing to do except sit in a chair. Then I saw you spring to your feet. I thought you wanted to talk to me but you ran to the phone and called a friend to get the latest gossip. I watched as you went to work and I waited patiently all day long. With all your activities I guess you were too busy to say anything to me.

I noticed that before lunch you looked around, maybe you felt embarrassed to talk to me, that is why you didn't bow your head. You glanced three or four tables over and you noticed some of your friends talking to me briefly before they ate, but you didn't. That's OK. There is still more time left, and I have hope that you will talk to me and yet you went home and it seems as if you had lots of things to do.

After a few of them were done you turned on the TV. I don't know if you like TV or not, just about anything goes there and you spend a lot of time each day in front of it, not thinking about anything — just enjoying the programme.

I waited patiently again as you watched the TV and ate your meal but again you didn't talk to me. Bedtime I guess you felt too tired. After you said goodnight to your family you flopped into bed and fell asleep in no time. That's OK because you may not realise that I am always there for you. I've got patience more than you will ever know. I even want to teach you how to be patient with others as well. I love you so much that I will wait every day for a nod, prayer or thought or a thankful part of your heart.

It is hard to have a one-sided conversation. Well, you are getting up again and once again I will wait with nothing but love for you hoping that today you will give me some time. Have a nice day!

Your friend,

GOD

After his cat got stuck up a tree, a vicar mounted a rescue operation. He climbed a ladder, tied one end of a rope to the narrow trunk, and the other end to the tow bar of his car. He gently drove forward and the inevitable occurred: the rope snapped, catapaulting (sorry!) the cat into the sky.

No more was heard of the cat until a few weeks later. The vicar went to visit a member of his church, a young mum (and her little boy, Johnny). In her front room, lying on the rug, was the vicar's cat! 'How did you find such a lovely cat?' the vicar asked, with thinly disguised innocence.

'You'll never believe it,' replied the mother. 'My little Johnny's been asking for a cat for months. In the end I got so tired of it I told him to come out in the garden where I was hanging out the washing. I told him the only thing to do was to pray. So we put our hands together and looked to the heavens. "Dear Jesus," we prayed, "please send us a pussy cat." And you'll never guess what happened next, Vicar....'

Preachers

There was a preacher who lost his voice on a Saturday night, just after he had prepared the best sermon of his life. His assistant said, 'You sit at the bottom of the stairs and whisper words and I'll go into the pulpit and proclaim them.'

'Moses was an austere man.'
'Moses was an oyster man!'

'And he made an atonement for the sins of the people.'
'And he made some toe ointment for the shins of the people!'

'You silly fool, you've gone and spoilt it all.'
'Then the silly fool went and spilt it all!'

Preaching

 Another hindrance of God's people is hardness of heart caused by hearing men without the Spirit preach about the Spirit.
A W Tozer

Old Gladys attended a church service one particular Sunday. The sermon seemed to go on for ever, and many in the congregation fell asleep.

After the service, to be social, she walked up to a very sleepy looking gentleman, and in an attempt to revive him from his stupor, extended her hand in greeting and said, 'Hello, I'm Gladys Dunn.'

To which the gentleman replied, 'You're not the only one!'

After the church service a little boy told the pastor, 'When I grow up, I'm going to give you some money.'

'Well, thank you,' the pastor replied, 'but why?'

'Because my daddy says you're one of the poorest preachers we've ever had.'

A suggested prayer for all preachers: 'Lord, fill my mouth with worthwhile stuff and nudge me when I've said enough.'

Preachers should remember that the capacity of the mind to absorb is limited to what the seat can endure.

A preacher usually takes a text and preaches from it — very far from it.

If some people preached what they practised it would have to be censored.

Every Christian occupies some kind of pulpit and preaches some kind of sermon every day.

Prejudice

'Some minds are like concrete, thoroughly mixed up and permanently set.'

J. John

Don't air your prejudices. Smother them.

Priorities

One day an expert was speaking to a group of business students and, to drive home a point, used an illustration those students would never forget.

As this man stood in front of the group of high-powered over-achievers, he said, 'OK, time for a quiz.'

Then he pulled out a one-gallon, wide-mouthed mason jar and set it on a table in front of him. Then he produced about a dozen fist-sized rocks and carefully placed them, one at a time, into the jar.

When the jar was filled to the top and no more rocks would fit inside, he asked, 'Is this jar full?'

Everyone in the class said, 'Yes.'

Then he said, 'Really?' He reached under the table and pulled out a bucket of gravel. Then he dumped some gravel in and shook the jar causing pieces of gravel to work themselves down into the spaces between the big rocks.

Then he asked the group once more, 'Is the jar full?'

By this time the class was onto him. 'Probably not,' one of them answered.

'Good!' he replied.

He reached under the table and brought out a bucket of sand. He started dumping the sand in and it went into all the spaces left between the rocks and the gravel. Once more he asked the question, 'Is this jar full?'

'No!' the class shouted. Once again he said, 'Good!' Then he grabbed a pitcher of water and began to pour it in until the jar was filled to the brim. Then he looked up at the class and asked, 'What is the point of this illustration?'

One eager beaver raised his hand and said, 'The point is, no matter how full your schedule is, if you try really hard, you can always fit some more things into it!'

'No,' the speaker replied, 'that's not the point. The truth this illustration teaches us is: If you don't put the big rocks in first, you'll never get them in at all.'

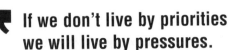

If we don't live by priorities we will live by pressures.

J. John

Progress

An Amish boy and his father were visiting a shopping mall. They were amazed by almost everything they saw, but especially by two shiny, silver walls that could move apart and back together again. The boy asked, 'What is this, Father?' The father (never having seen a lift) responded, 'Son, I have never seen anything like this in my life, I don't know what it is.'

While the boy and his father were watching with amazement, an old lady in a wheelchair rolled up to the moving walls and pressed a button. The walls opened and the lady rolled between them into a small room. The walls closed and the boy and his father watched the small circular numbers above the walls light up sequentially. They continued to watch until it reached the last number and then as these numbers began to light in reverse order. The walls opened up again and a beautiful twenty-four-year-old woman stepped out.

The father, not taking his eyes off the young woman, said quietly to his son, 'Quick! Go and get your mother.'

'The test of progress is not whether we add more to the abundance of those who have much; it is whether we provide enough for those who have too little.'

Franklin D Roosevelt

We trained hard — but it seemed that every time we were beginning to form up into teams, we would be reorganised. I was to learn later in life that we tend to meet any new situation by reorganising, and a wonderful method it can be for creating the illusion of progress while producing confusion, inefficiency and demoralisation.

Gaius Petronius, AD 66

Questions

If quitters never win, and winners never quit, what fool came up with, 'Quit while you're ahead'?

Do Lipton employees take coffee breaks?

How much deeper would oceans be if sponges didn't live there?

If it's true that we are here to help others, then what exactly are the OTHERS here for?

If a man says something in the woods and there are no women there, is he still wrong?

Ever wonder what the speed of lightning would be if it didn't zig-zag?

If a person with multiple personalities threatens suicide, is that considered a hostage situation?

If olive oil comes from olives, where does baby oil come from?

Why don't they just make mouse-flavoured cat food?

If you're sending someone some Styrofoam, what do you pack it in?

Why do they sterilise needles for lethal injections?

Whose cruel idea was it for the word 'lisp' to have an 's' in it?

How come abbreviated is such a long word?

Why do you press harder on a remote-control when you know the battery is dead?

Why are they called buildings, when they're already finished? Shouldn't they be called builts?

If men and women evolved from monkeys and apes, why do we still have monkeys and apes?

Isn't it a bit unnerving that doctors call what they do 'practice'?

Would a fly without wings be called a walk?

If the police arrest a mime artist, does he or she still have the right to remain silent?

Before they invented drawing boards, what did they go back to?

How do I set my laser printer on stun?

How is it possible to have a civil war?

If all the world is a stage, where is the audience sitting?

If one synchronised swimmer drowns, do the rest have to drown too?

If you try to fail, and succeed, which have you done?

If the black box flight recorder is never damaged during a plane crash, why isn't the whole aeroplane made out of the stuff?

Questioning

It is easier to judge a person's mental capacity by their questions than by their answers.

'Don't be afraid to ask dumb questions. They are easier to handle than dumb mistakes.'
Thomas Fuller

To question a wise person is wisdom.

Not every question deserves an answer.

Quiet

'An inability to stay quiet is one of the most conspicuous failures of human kind.'
Walter Bagehot

Silence is evidence of a superb command of the English language.

Quotes

What you are is God's gift to you. What you become is your gift to God.

Do your best and then sleep in peace. God is awake.

The will of God will never take you to where the grace of God will not protect you.

We set the sail; God makes the wind.

The task ahead of us is never as great as the power behind us.

Serenity is not freedom from the storm, but peace amid the storm.

Follow your dream! Unless it's the one where you're at work in your underwear during a fire drill.

Religion

A Protestant moved into a completely Catholic community. Being good Catholics they welcomed him into their community. But, also because they were good Catholics they did not eat red meat on Fridays. So when their neighbour began barbecuing some juicy steak on Friday night, they began to squirm. They were so annoyed that they went to talk to him about it. After much talk they convinced him to become a Catholic.

The next Sunday he went to the priest and the priest sprinkled holy water on him and said, 'You were born Protestant. You were raised Protestant. But now you are Catholic.'

And so, the next Friday, as the neighbours sat down to eat their fish, they were disturbed by the smell of roast beef coming from the neighbouring house. They went over to talk to the new Catholic because he knew he was not supposed to eat beef on Fridays. When they saw him, he was sprinkling ketchup on the beef saying, 'You were born a cow. You were raised a cow. But now you are fish.'

Remembrance

In an ancient monastery in a faraway place, a new monk arrived to join his brothers in copying books and scrolls in the monastery's scriptorium. His job was to copy the copies.

One day, he asked Father Florian (the rather ancient head of the scriptorium), 'Does not the copying by hand of other copies allow for error? How do we know we are not copying the mistakes of someone else? Are they ever checked against the original?'

Father Florian was taken aback by the observation of this youthful monk. 'A very good point, my son. I will take one of the latest books down to the vault and compare it against the original.'

Father Florian went down to the vault and began his verification. After a day had passed, the monks began to worry and went down looking for the old priest. They were sure something must have happened. As they approached the vault, they heard crying. When they opened the door, they found Father Florian sobbing over the new copy and the original ancient book, both of which were opened before him on the table. It was obvious to all that the poor man had been crying his heart out for a long time.

'What is the problem, Reverend Father?' asked one of the monks.

'Oh dear, oh dear,' sobbed the priest. 'In the ancient book of the sacred rites of priesthood... the word is "CELEBRATE"!'

Repentance

A sneak thief who turned to God has cleared his guilty conscience by returning stolen property he took five years ago, wrote John Davison of *The Sunday Times*. Last week the man replaced a stolen personal stereo with a new one and added £20 compensation. A note in the package, handed to his victim in Greater Manchester, said that he had found the Lord. The thief added that the Lord had forgiven him and that he wanted the family to forgive him too.

'We couldn't believe it after all this time,' said Sue Marshall, forty-eight, 'We don't know who the thief is, but we want him to know that we do forgive him.'

A police spokesman said: 'It would be nice if a few more thieves around here had similar pangs of conscience.'

One of the most popular books in the late 1990s was entitled *What They Don't Teach You at Harvard Business School*. This is now regarded as a classic in the business fraternity. The book proposed that there are three things you are not taught that you desperately need to say:

1. I'm wrong
2. I'm sorry
3. Please help me.

Unless you say (1) you'll never move on in business. Unless you say (2) you'll be arrogant. Unless you say (3) your self-sufficiency will be your downfall.

Restlessness

Boris Becker, the noted tennis player came close to taking his own life through being overwhelmed by a sense of hopelessness and emptiness.

'I have won Wimbledon twice before, once as the youngest player. I was rich, I had all the material possessions I needed — money, cars, women, everything. I know that this is a cliché, it's the old song of the movie and pop stars who commit suicide. They have everything and yet they are so unhappy. I had no inner peace. I was a puppet on a string.'

Resurrection

A vicar once went on his own for a walking holiday in the Lakes. He befriended a young shepherd lad who asked him to explain the Christian faith to him. The vicar pointed to the fingers of his right hand and said, pointing to each finger, 'The Lord is *my* shepherd.' As he said this, he emphasised the word *my* and held onto the fourth finger of his right hand. 'The important thing,' he said, is to be able to say that 'the Lord is *my* shepherd.'

The following summer the vicar went back to the same place. He couldn't find the boy anywhere and was sad. One day he came across a farmhouse and decided to knock on the door for a drink. The owner let him into the kitchen for a cup of tea. As he looked around his eyes alighted on a photograph on the mantle piece above the kitchen fire. There was the boy! So the vicar asked the woman of the house about him. 'Oh, that was my son,' she replied. 'He died last winter during a very severe blizzard. In fact they brought his body here into the kitchen and laid it on this very table. It was a horrible moment. One thing was a bit strange though. My son was holding onto the fourth finger of his right hand...'

There were two nextdoor neighbours. One neighbour goes away on holiday and asks the other neighbour to look after their house and garden. They go round to the house and do the garden, taking their dog with them.

After a few minutes the dog comes running to the owners with a rabbit in its mouth. They catch the dog, retrieve the rabbit and find that it's dead and slightly chewed! They just can't believe it.

They think 'Oh, no, what shall we do?' They brush the rabbit and get the hairdryer and try to do its hair and dry it and then put it back in its rabbit hutch. The neighbours who were on holiday return the day after and they ask their friends, 'Did anything unusual happen in our garden while we were away?' The others reply, 'No, why do you ask?' 'Well, it's ever so strange but our rabbit died the day before we left for our holiday and we buried it... !'

Three friends die in a car crash, and go to an orientation meeting in heaven. During this orientation, they are all asked, 'When you are in your coffin and friends and family are mourning you, what would you like to hear them say about you?'

The first man says, 'I would like to hear them say that I was a great doctor of my time and a great family man.'

The second says, 'I would like to hear that I was a wonderful husband and school teacher who made a huge difference to the children of tomorrow.'

The last replies, 'I would like to hear them say, "Look, he's moving!"'

Revelation

**'I want to know God's thoughts...
the rest are details.'**

Albert Einstein

S

Satisfaction

> *Taste the sweetness of God who alone can satisfy our deepest hunger.*
> **Delia Smith**

The strange thing is that people are satisfied with so little in themselves but demand so much of others.

Sacrifice

On Sunday, 16 August 1987, Northwest Airlines flight 225 crashed just after taking off from Detroit Airport. One hundred and fifty-five people were killed. One survived: a four-year-old from Tempe, Arizona, named Cecelia.

News accounts say when rescuers found Cecelia they did not believe she had been on the plane. Investigators first assumed Cecelia had been a passenger in one of the cars on the highway onto which the airliner crashed. But when the passenger register for the flight was checked, there was Cecelia's name.

Cecelia survived because, as the plane was falling, Cecelia's mother, Paula Chican, unbuckled her own seat belt, got down on her knees in front of her daughter, wrapped her arms and body around Cecelia, and then would not let her go.

Nothing could separate that child from her parent's love — not tragedy or disaster, not the fall or the flames that followed, not height nor depth, not life nor death. Such is the love of our Saviour for us. He left heaven, lowered himself to us, and covered us with the sacrifice of his own body to save us.

Salvation

 If you have an accident, you are qualified for an ambulance. If you have a cancer, you are qualified for a hospital. If you are a sinner, you are qualified for a Saviour.

Science

In our modern world many people feel that our rapid advances in the field of science render such things as religious belief old-fashioned. They wonder why we should be satisfied in believing something when science tells us that we know so many things. The answer to this is that we are faced with many more mysteries today than when the scientific age began. With every new answer science has discovered more questions. These answers indicate that anything so perfectly created as our earth and universe must have had a maker, a master designer. Anything so orderly, so perfect, so precisely balanced, so majestic as this creation can only be the product of a divine idea. That is one reason why I am a Christian. (Secondly, he revealed himself in Jesus).

Former Director of NASA, **Werner Von Braun**

Second coming

'Don't worry about the world coming to an end today. It's already tomorrow in Australia.'
Charles Schultz

A few years ago an eccentric called Ernest Digweed died leaving £26,107 in his estate. He left it to Jesus Christ on his return to earth. His will reads:

If during the eighty years after my death the Lord Jesus Christ shall come to reign on earth, then the public trustee, upon obtaining proof of his identity, shall pay to the Lord Jesus Christ all the property which he holds on behalf of the estate.

There are apparently at least two files of letters from people making claims to this money. The government officer looking after them says, 'They tend to be from rather eccentric types lacking in humour.'

Self-discipline

Dear Lord, so far today I've done all right. I haven't gossiped, lost my temper, been nasty, greedy, overbearing, selfish or obnoxious. I'm really glad I've accomplished all these things on my own. But in a few minutes, Lord, I'm going to have to get out of bed — and from that point on I'm going to need all the help I can get from you. Amen.

Selflessness

There are two seas in Palestine. One is fresh, and fish are in it. Splashes of green adorn its banks. Trees spread their branches over it and stretch out their thirsty roots to sip of its healing waters. Along its shores the children play, as children played when he was there. He loved it. He could look across its silver surface when Jesus spoke his parables. And on a rolling plain not far away he fed five thousand people.

The River Jordan makes this sea with sparkling water from the hills. So it laughs in the sunshine. And men build their houses near to it, and birds their nests; and every kind of life is happier because it is there.

The River Jordan flows on south into another sea. Here is no splash of fish, no fluttering leaf, no song of birds, no children's laughter. Travellers choose another route, unless on urgent business. The air hangs heavy above its water, and neither man nor beast nor fowl will drink.

What makes this mighty difference in these neighbour seas? Not the River Jordan. It empties the same good water into both. Not the soil in which they lie, not the country about.

This is the difference. The Sea of Galilee receives but does not keep the Jordan. For every drop that flows into it another drop flows out. The giving and receiving go on in equal measure.

The other sea is shrewder, hoarding its income jealously. It will not be tempted into any generous impulse. Every drop it gets, it keeps.

The Sea of Galilee gives and lives. This other sea gives nothing. It is named The Dead. There are two kinds of people in the world. There are two seas in Palestine.

Gayle D. Erwin

Sensitivity

Phil goes to Europe and leaves his favourite dog with his brother James. While in Europe, Phil calls James to check on his dog and asks, 'So James, how's my favourite dog doing?'

James very tersely says, 'Your dog is dead.'

'What?' says Phil, 'You can't just tell someone his favourite dog is dead without warning. You have to ease him into it.'

'How?' says James.

'Well, the first day I call, tell me my dog is on the roof,' remarked Phil, 'Tell me the dog is going to be fine and not to worry. The next day, when I call to ask about my dog, tell me that you were about to get her down, when she jumped off the roof and broke her leg. Tell me the doctors say the dog will be OK, but it will have to stay at the vet's for a while. Are you getting all of this?'

'Yes,' says James.

'Good,' remarks Phil. 'Then the next day, when I call back, tell me that there was severe internal bleeding that the vet didn't pick up, and that my favourite dog died at 2am this morning. That way it won't be such a shock to me. Got it?'

'Yes.'

'Good, so how's Grandma doing?' asks Phil.

'Well,' James replies, 'She's on the roof...'

Service

> 'Dear Lord, do not make us like porridge, which is difficult to stir and slow to serve. But more like Corn Flakes, crisp, fresh and ready to serve.'
>
> **(Boy's Brigade, camp grace)**

When Apollo Mission Astronaut Neil Armstrong first walked on the moon, he not only gave his famous 'one small step for man, one giant leap for mankind' statement, but followed it by several remarks. Mostly routine conversation with the other astronauts.

Just before he re-entered the lunar lander, however, he made the enigmatic remark, 'Good luck, Mr Gorsky.'

Many people at NASA thought it was a casual remark concerning some rival Soviet cosmonaut. However, upon checking, there was no Gorsky in either the Russian or American space programs.

Over the years many people questioned Armstrong as to what the 'Good luck, Mr Gorsky' statement meant, but Armstrong always just smiled and dodged the question.

On 5 July 1995 in Tampa Bay, Florida, while answering questions following a speech, a reporter brought up the twenty-six-year-old question to Armstrong. This time he finally responded. Mr Gorsky had finally died and so Neil Armstrong felt he could answer the question.

When he was a child, he was playing baseball with a friend in the back garden. His friend hit a fly ball, which landed in the front of his neighbour's bedroom windows. His neighbours were Mr and Mrs Gorsky.

As he leaned down to pick up the ball, young Armstrong heard Mrs Gorsky shouting at Mr Gorsky. 'Sex! You want sex?! You'll get sex when the kid next door walks on the moon!'

True story!

A man doing market research knocked on a door and was greeted by a young woman with three small children running around at her feet. He said, 'I'm doing some research for Vaseline. Have you ever used the product?'

She said, 'Yes. My husband and I use it all the time.'

'And if you don't mind me asking, what do you use it for?'

'We use it for sex.'

The researcher was a little taken aback. He said, 'Usually people lie to me and say that they use it on a child's bicycle chain or to help with a gate hinge. But, in fact, I know that most people do use it for sex. I admire you for your honesty. Since you've been frank so far, can you tell me exactly how you use it for sex?'

The woman said, 'I don't mind telling you at all. My husband and I put it on the door knob and it keeps the kids out.'

The minister was passing a group of young teenagers sitting on the church lawn and stopped to ask what they were doing. 'Nothing much, Pastor,' replied one lad. 'We're just seeing who can tell the biggest lie about their sex life.'

'Boys! Boys! Boys!' he intoned. 'I'm shocked. Why, when I was your age I never even thought about sex at all.'

They all replied, pretty much in unison, 'You win, Pastor!'

A honeymoon couple arrive at their hotel room and they find two beds. The wife changes and gets into one bed and the husband changes and gets into the other bed.

She says, 'Oh, I am cold!' So the husband gets out of bed and he removes a blanket from his bed and puts it onto hers.

He gets back into bed.

She says, 'Oh, I am cold!' So he gets out, pulls the sheet off his bed and puts that on her bed and gets back into his bed.

She says, 'Oh, I am cold!'

He says, 'Well, there's nothing else I can give you from my bed.'

And she says, 'Well, when I was younger, my mother used to come into my bed and cuddle me.'

So he starts to put his clothes on and says, 'OK then, I'll get your mum.'

Sharing

A mother was preparing pancakes for her sons, Kevin, five, and Ryan, three. The boys began to argue over who would get the first pancake. Their mother saw the opportunity for a moral lesson.

'If Jesus were sitting here, he would say, "Let my brother have the first pancake, I can wait."'

Kevin turned to his younger brother and said, 'Ryan, you be Jesus!'

Shocks

An archaeologist was digging in the Negev Desert in Israel and came upon a coffin containing a mummy. After examining it, he called the curator of a prestigious natural-history museum. 'I've just discovered a 3,000-year-old mummy of a man who died of heart failure!' the excited scientist exclaimed.

To which the curator replied, 'Bring him in. We'll check it out.'

A week later, the amazed curator called the archaeologist. 'You were right about the mummy's age and cause of death. How in the world did you know?'

'Easy. There was a piece of paper in his hand that said, "10,000 shekels on Goliath".'

Shopping

Tesco ergo sum:
   I shop therefore I am
Veni, Vidi, Visa:
   I came, I saw, I shopped.

Signs of the Times

The following anonymous reflection sums up contemporary culture very well:

We have taller buildings but shorter tempers

Wider motorways but narrower viewpoints

We spend more, but we have less

We buy more, but enjoy it less

We have bigger houses and smaller families

More conveniences, but less time

We have more degrees, but less common sense

More knowledge, but less judgement

More experts, but more problems

More medicine, but less well being

We have multiplied our possessions, but reduced our values

We talk too much, but lie too often

We've learned how to make a living, but not how to live life

We have added years to life, but not life to years

We've been all the way to the moon and back, but can't cross the street to help a neighbour

We write more, but learn less

We plan more, but accomplish less

We have higher incomes, but lower morals

We have more acquaintances but fewer friends

These are times of fast foods and slow digestion

Tall men and short character

Steep profits and shallow relationships

These are times of world peace but domestic warfare

More leisure and less fun

More kinds of food but less nutrition

These are days of two incomes but more divorce

Of fancier houses but broken homes

It is a time when there is much in the shop window and nothing in the stock room.

(Abridged and amended.)
Anon.

Have you heard about the new psychiatric hot-line? When you phone in you get this message:

- If you are obsessive-compulsive, please press 1 repeatedly.
- If you are co-dependent, please ask someone else to press 2.
- If you have multiple personalities, please press 3, 4, 5 and 6.
- If you are paranoid-delusional, we know who you are and what you want. Just stay on the line so that we can trace your call.
- If you are schizophrenic, listen carefully and a little voice will tell you which number to press.
- If you are manic-depressive, it doesn't matter which number you press. No one will answer.

Anon.

Simplicity

The Canadians wanted to find a writing implement that could be used in space.

It took 200 engineers and they spent over $2 billion to invent a space pen. This pen could write in zero gravity and the ink would still flow. The Canadians proudly announced their success and congratulations flowed in from all over the world.

In a short note to the Canadians, NASA congratulated them, but said that they too had found a solution at a fraction of the cost. They remarked, 'We use a pencil.'

Sin

'Sin is the most expensive thing in the universe… If it is forgiven sin, it cost God his only Son… If it is unforgiven sin, it costs the sinner his soul and an eternity in hell!' **Charles G Finney**

T he story behind the painting of the Last Supper is extremely interesting and instructive.

Two incidents connected with this painting afford a most convincing lesson on the effects of thought in the life of a boy or girl, or of a man or woman.

The Last Supper was painted by Leonardo Da Vinci, a noted Italian artist. The time engaged for its completion was seven years. The figures representing the twelve apostles and Christ himself were painted from living persons. The live model for the painting of the figure of Jesus was chosen first. When it was decided that Da Vinci would paint this great picture, hundreds and hundreds of young men were carefully viewed in an endeavour to find a face and personality completely devoid of dissipation caused by sin.

Finally, after weeks of laborious searching, a young man, nineteen years of age, was selected as the model for the portrayal of Christ. For six months Da Vinci worked on the production of this leading character of the famous painting.

During the next six years Da Vinci continued his labours on his sublime work of art. One by one, fitting persons were chosen to represent each of the eleven apostles, space being left for the painting of the figure representing Judas Iscariot as the final task of this masterpiece. This was the apostle, you remember, who betrayed his Lord for thirty pieces of silver.

For weeks Da Vinci searched for a man with a hard callous face, with a countenance marked by scars of avarice and deceit, who would betray his best friend. After many discouraging experiences in searching for the type of person required to represent Judas, word came to Da Vinci that a man whose appearance fully met the requirements had been found. He was in a dungeon in Rome, sentenced to die for a life of crime and murder. Da Vinci made the trip to Rome at once, and this man was brought out from his imprisonment in the dungeon and led out into the light of the sun. There Da Vinci saw before him a dark, swarthy man, his long shaggy and unkempt hair sprawled over his face. A face which portrayed a character of viciousness and complete ruin. At last the painter had found the person he wanted to represent the character of Judas in his painting.

By special permission from the king, this prisoner was carried to Milan where the fresco was being painted. For six months the prisoner sat before Da Vinci, at appointed hours each day, as the gifted artist diligently continued his task of transmitting to his painting this base character in the picture representing the traitor and betrayer of the Saviour.

As he finished his last stroke, he turned to the guards and said, 'I have finished, you may take the prisoner away. He suddenly broke loose from their control and rushed up to Da Vinci, crying as he did so. 'Oh, Da Vinci, look at me! Do you not know who I am?'

Da Vinci, with the trained eyes of a great character student, carefully scrutinised the man upon whose face he had constantly gazed for six months and replied; 'No, I have never seen you in my life until you were brought before me out of the dungeon in Rome.' Then lifting his eyes toward heaven, the prisoner sad, 'O God, have I fallen so low?'

Then, turning his face to the painter, he said, 'Leonardo Da Vinci, look at me again, for I am the same man you painted just seven years ago as the figure of Christ!'

This is the true story of the painting of the Last Supper that teaches so strongly the lesson of the effects of right and wrong thinking of an individual. He was a young man whose character was so pure and unspoiled by the sins of the world that he represented a countenance and innocence and beauty fit to be used for the painting of a representation of Christ. But during the seven years, following a life of sin and crime, he was changed into a perfect picture of the most notorious character ever known in the history of the world.

Anon.

> 'There are two kinds of people: the just, who consider themselves sinners, and the sinners, who consider themselves just.'
>
> **Pascal**, *Pensees*, 1670

Nine modern-day sins

- Booking a table in a restaurant and not turning up.
- Taking coat hangers from hotels.
- Pledging money for a telethon, but not sending it.
- Not clearing away your tray at McDonalds.
- Taking ten items through the nine items or less checkouts.
- Starting the bottom layer of a chocolate box before finishing the top layer.
- Unfolding all the sweaters in Benetton.
- Phoning your cousin in Australia from work.

Society

For those born before 1940…

You were born before television, before penicillin, polio shots, frozen foods, Xerox, plastic, contact lenses, videos, Frisbees and the Pill. You were born before radar, credit cards, split atoms, laser beams and ball-point pens; before dishwashers, tumble driers, electric blankets, air conditioners, drip-dry clothes… and before man walked on the moon.

You got married first and then lived together. You thought 'fast food' was what you ate in Lent, a 'Big Mac' an oversized raincoat and 'crumpet' something you had for tea. You existed before house-husbands, computer dating, dual careers, and when a 'meaningful relationship' meant getting along with cousins and 'sheltered accommodation' was where you waited for a bus.

You were born before day-care centres, group homes and disposable nappies. You never heard of FM radio, tape decks, electric typewriters, artificial hearts, word processors, yogurt and young men wearing earings. For you 'time sharing' meant togetherness, a 'chip' was a piece of wood or a fried potato, 'hardware' meant nuts and bolts and 'software' was not a word.

Before 1940, 'Made in Japan' meant junk, the term 'making out' referred to how you did in your exams, 'stud' was something that fastened a collar to a shirt, and 'going all the way' meant staying on a double-decker bus to the bus depot. Pizzas, McDonalds and instant coffee were unheard of. In your day cigarette smoking was 'fashionable'; 'grass' was mown, 'coke' was kept in the coal house, a 'joint' was a piece of meat you had on Sundays and 'pot' was something you cooked in. 'Rock music' was a grandmother's lullaby. 'Eldorado' was an ice cream, a 'gay' person was the life and soul of the party and nothing more, while 'AIDS' just meant beauty treatment or help from someone in trouble.

Statistics

Some figures for the year 2000 collected by American missions statistician David B Barrett:

- Of the global population of 6,091,351,000: 2,015,743,000 believe in Christianity in some form.
- 1.898 billion are members of Christian churches, 1.3 billion attend Christian services.
- 482 million belong to Pentecostal or Charismatic movements, some 680 million are 'Great Commission Christians'.
- In the year 2000, 165,000 will probably be martyred for their faith.
- There are 24,000 missions organisations which collect some US$120 billion per year.
- The total income of all church members is around US$12,700 billion, of which $220 billion are spent on Christian purposes.
- There are 5,104 million people in full-time ministry
- The 4,000 Christian radio and TV stations reach a total of 2.15 billion people.
- 2 billion people live in poor urban areas, 1.3 billion of them in slums.
- There are 4,100 cities with over 100,000 inhabitants, 410 cities with over 1 million other religions and groups: 1.215 billion Muslims, 786 million Hindus, 774 million non-religious, 362 million Buddhists, 225 million members of tribal religions, 151 million atheists, 102 million 'new religious'.

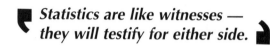

Statistics are like witnesses — they will testify for either side.

Stealing

In 1996 (Sunday 11 June), three thieves broke into a boat and started to rifle through all the items in it. They placed valuables in a swag bag and threw what they regarded as useless overboard. One of the things they threw overboard was a water-activated distress beacon. This went off as soon as it hit the sea and was picked up by a US weather satellite 550 miles directly above their heads. The satellite sent an SOS signal to the Inverness police who rushed to the scene and arrested the three very unwise men!

Stress

Grant me the serenity to accept the things I cannot change,
The courage to change the things I cannot accept,
And the wisdom to hide the bodies
Of those I had to kill today because they got on my nerves.

Also, help me to be careful of the toes I step on today
As they may be connected to the feet I may have to kiss tomorrow.
Help me always to give 100% at work:

17% on Monday
23% on Tuesday
30% on Wednesday
20% on Thursday
10% on Friday

And help me to remember:

When I'm having a bad day and it seems that
People are trying to wind me up:
It takes forty-two muscles to frown, twenty-eight to smile, and only four
To extend my arm and hit someone!

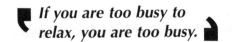

If you are too busy to relax, you are too busy.

Substitution

One day, a man went to visit a church. He arrived early, parked his car, and got out. Another car pulled up near him, and the driver told him, 'I always park there. You took my place!'

The visitor went inside for Sunday school, found an empty seat, and sat down. A young lady from the church approached him and stated, 'That's my seat! You took my place!'

The visitor was somewhat distressed by this rude welcome, but said nothing.

After Sunday school, the visitor went into the church sanctuary and sat down. Another member walked up to him and said, 'That's where I always sit. You took my place!'

The visitor was even more troubled by this treatment, but still said nothing.

Later, as the congregation was praying for Christ to dwell among them, the visitor stood, and his appearance began to change. Horrible scars became visible on his hands and on his sandalled feet. Someone from the congregation noticed him and called out, 'What happened to you?'

The visitor replied, 'I took your place.'

In an interview, actor Kevin Bacon shared a conversation he had with his six-year-old son after he'd seen the movie *Footloose* for the first time. The boy said, 'Dad, that was really cool, how you jumped up on the roof and swung from the rafters. How did you do that?'

'Well son, I didn't actually do that part,' said Bacon. 'A stunt man did.' 'What's a stunt man?' asked his son.

'That's someone who dresses like me and does things that I can't do. Things that are too dangerous.'

'Oh well, what about that part in the movie where you spin around on the gym bar and land on your feet,' persisted the boy. 'How did you do that?'

'Well son, that was the stunt man again, not me. He's really good at gymnastics.'

'Oh.' A long pause. 'Dad, just what did you do in the movie?'

Bacon sheepishly replied, 'I got all the glory.'

Teachers

A school teacher injured his back and had to wear a plaster cast around the upper part of his body. It fitted under his shirt and was not noticeable at all.

On the first day of term, still with the cast under his shirt, he found himself assigned to the toughest students in school. Walking confidently into the rowdy classroom, he opened the window as wide as possible and then busied himself with desk work. When a strong breeze made his tie flap, he took the desk stapler and stapled the tie to his chest.

Discipline was not a problem from that day forth!

A teacher who was lecturing on habits told his class that 'anything you repeat twenty times is yours for ever.' From the back of the classroom came a whispered voice, 'Mandy. Mandy. Mandy. Mandy...'

The teacher gave her class some homework: Get their parents to tell them a story with a moral at the end of it. The next day the children came back and one by one began to tell their stories. Kathy said, 'My father's a farmer and we have a lot of egg-laying hens. One time we were taking our eggs to market in a basket on the front seat of the van when we hit a bump in the road and all the eggs went flying and broke and made a mess.'

'And what's the moral of the story?' asked the teacher.

'Don't put all your eggs in one basket!'

'Very good,' said the teacher.

Next little Lucy raised a hand and said, 'Our family are farmers too. But we rear chickens for the poultry market. We had a dozen eggs once, but when they hatched we only got ten live chicks and the moral to this story is, don't count your chickens until they're hatched.'

'That was a fine story, Lucy. Jack, do you have a story to share?'

'Yes, my dad told me this story about my Aunt Karen. Aunt Karen was a flight engineer in Desert Storm and her plane was hit. She had to bail out over enemy territory and all she had was a bottle of whisky, a machine gun and a machete. She drank the whisky on the way down so it wouldn't break and then she landed right in the middle of 100 enemy troops. She killed seventy of them with the machine gun until she ran out of bullets, then she killed twenty more with the machete till the blade broke and then she killed the last ten with her bare hands.'

'Good heavens,' said the horrified teacher, 'what kind of moral did your father teach you from that horrible story?'

'Don't hassle Aunt Karen when she's been drinking.'

Television

The Twenty-third Channel

The TV is my shepherd, I shall not want.
It makes me lie down on the sofa
It leads me away from the faith
It destroys my soul
It leads me in the paths of sex and violence
For the sponsors' sake.
Yea, though I walk in the shadow of my responsibilities
There will be no interruption
For the TV is with me,
Its cable and remote control
They comfort me.
It prepares a commercial before me
In the presence of my worldliness.
It anoints my head with humanism and consumerism.
My covetousness runneth over.
Surely laziness and ignorance
Shall follow me all the days of my life
And I shall dwell in the house
Watching TV for ever.

Time

Yesterday was history,
Tomorrow is a mystery,
Today is a gift of God,
That is why it's called the PRESENT.

You can run several agenda in life, but you cannot run them all at a hundred per cent without someone paying the price. We have so many excuses. The main one is that we convince ourselves that a slower day is coming. We say to ourselves, 'When the house is decorated, when I get my promotion, when I pass those exams — then I'll have more time.' Every time we have to say, 'Not now, darling...' we tell ourselves it's OK because that slower day is getting nearer. It's as well that we realise, here and now, that the slower day is an illusion — it never comes. Whatever our situation, we all have the potential to fill up our time. That's why we need to make time for the things that we believe are important — and we need to make it now.

Rob Parsons

The Lord is my pacesetter, I need not rush,
He makes me stop and rest for quiet intervals.
He provides me with images of stillness, which restore my serenity.
He leads me in ways of efficiency through calmness of mind.
His guidance is peace.
Even though I have a great deal of things to accomplish each day, I will not fret.
For his presence is here, his timelessness, his importance will keep me in balance.
He prepares refreshment and renewal in the midst of activity
by anointing my head with oils of tranquility.
My cup of joyous energy overflows.
Such harmony and effectiveness shall be the fruit of my hours,
For I shall walk in the peace of the Lord
And dwell in his company for ever. Amen.

(Toki Miyamisha's version of Psalm 23)

Tiredness

Five best things to say if you get caught sleeping at your desk:

5. They told me at the blood bank this might happen.
4. Whew! I must have left the top off the Tipex. You probably got here just in time!
3. I wasn't sleeping! I was meditating on the vision statement and envisioning a new paradigm.
2. I was testing my keyboard for drool resistance.
1. … in Jesus' name. Amen.

Transformation

The Touch of The Master's Hand

'Twas battered and scarred, and
    the auctioneer
Thought it scarcely worth the while
To waste much time on the old
    violin,
But he held it up with a smile.

'What am I offered, good folks?' he
    cried,
'Who'll start the bidding for me?
A pound — a pound — now two,
    only two,
Two pounds, and who'll make it
    three?

'Going for three,' sang the
    auctioneer,
'Going for three —' but no,
From the back of the room an old
    grey-haired man
Came forward and picked up the
    bow.

Then, wiping the dust from the old
    violin
And tuning up all the strings,
He played a melody pure and
    sweet,
As sweet as an angel sings.

The music ceased, and the
    auctioneer
With a voice that was quiet and
    low
Said, 'What am I bid for the old
    violin?'
And held it up with the bow.

'A thousand pounds? And who'll
    make it two?
Two thousand, and who'll make it
    three?
Three thousand once, three
    thousand twice,
Going, and gone,' said he.

The people cheered, and some of
    them cried,
'We do not understand
What changed its worth?' a man
    replied,
'The touch of the master's hand.'

Many a man with life out of tune
And battered and torn with sin
Is auctioned cheap to a thoughtless
    crowd,
Much like the old violin.

A 'mess of pottage', a glass of
    wine,
A game, and he travels on.
He's going once, he's going
    twice —
He's going and almost gone.

But the master comes, and the
    foolish crowd
Never can quite understand
The worth of a soul,
And the change that is wrought
By the touch of the master's hand

Myra Brooks Welch

Triumph

> **Triumph is just UMPH added to TRY.**

U

Unity

There's a story about an American flying across the Atlantic to England. It was planting season, and when he looked down and saw the stone walls and the geometric designs in the English countryside, he thought it was so beautiful. He stayed in England for several months. Then, when he flew back to America, back across the same area, the walls were all gone. He asked the flight attendant what happened to the fences. She said, 'Oh sir, it's harvest time. The wheat is now higher than the walls, so you can't see them.'

During the great revivals in Northampton, USA, Jonathan Edwards and his people were so fearful of losing the blessing through division they made a community resolution:

1. In all our conversation, concerns, and dealings with our neighbours we will be honest, just and upright.
2. If we wrong others in any way we will not rest until we have made restitution.
3. We promise that we will not permit ourselves to indulge in any kind of back-biting.
4. We will be careful not to do anything to others out of a spirit of revenge.
5. When there is a difference of opinion concerning another's rights, we will not allow private interest to influence us.
6. We will not tolerate the exercise of enmity or ill will or revenge in our hearts.
7. If we find that we have a secret grudge against another we will not gratify it but root it out.
8. We will not allow over-familiarity in our talk with others, or anything that might stir up licentious behaviour.
9. We resolve to examine ourselves on a regular basis, knowing that the heart is very deceitful.
10. We will run with perseverance the race that is set before us, working out our salvation with fear and trembling.

This covenant was made on 16 March 1742

Verbosity

Sherlock Holmes and Dr Watson went on a camping trip. After a good meal and a bottle of wine they lay down for the night and went to sleep. Some hours later, Holmes awoke and nudged his faithful friend.

'Watson, look up at the sky and tell me what you see.'

Watson replied, 'I see millions and millions of stars.'

'What does that tell you?'

Watson pondered for a minute. 'Astronomically, it tells me that there are millions of galaxies and potentially billions of planets. Astrologically, I observe that Saturn is in Leo. Horologically, I deduce that the time is approximately a quarter past three. Theologically, I can see that God is all-powerful and that we are small and insignificant. Meteorologically, I suspect that we will have a beautiful day tomorrow. What does it tell you?'

Holmes was silent for a minute, then spoke. 'It tells me that some thief has stolen our tent.'

Pythagorean theorem: 24 words.
The Lord's prayer: 66 words.
Archimedes' Principle: 67 words.
The Ten Commandments: 179 words.
The Gettysburg address: 286 words.
The Declaration of Independence: 1,300 words.
US Government regulations on the sale of
    cabbage: 26,911 words.

Victory

In the original Olympic Games in ancient Greece, the greatest event was a race up and down mountains. Speed wasn't the most important issue, because the runners ran the race with a flaming torch. The winner was not necessarily the first person to reach the finishing line. It was the person who crossed the line with the flame still burning.

The moral? We need to run the race in such a way that we don't put out the flame. We might be later in crossing the line, not only because we are protecting our own flame but also because we are lighting the torches of others whose flame has gone out. Winning is about finishing well not finishing first.

Vision

A vision without a task is a dream. A task without a vision is drudgery. But the two together are the hope of the world.

A pile of rocks ceases to be a pile of rocks when somebody contemplates it with a cathedral in mind.

'Most people see no further than their noses.'

J. John

Some people who think they are dreamers are just sleepers.

At the opening of Disney World, Florida, Mrs Walt Disney gave the inaugural speech, her husband being dead. An interviewer said to her, 'I wish Dr Disney had lived to see it.'

Mrs Disney replied, 'He did.'

When a man with a vision meets a man with money, then the man with the money gets the vision, and the man with the vision gets the money.

'Eyes that look are common. Eyes that see are rare.'

J Oswald Sanders

When I was a young man, I wanted to change the world. I found it was difficult to change the world, so I tried to change my nation. When I found I couldn't change the nation, I began to focus on my town. I couldn't change the town and as an older man, I tried to change my family. Now, as an old man, I realise the only thing I can change is myself, and suddenly I realise that if long ago I had changed myself, I could have made an impact on my family. My family and I could have made an impact on our town. Their impact could have changed the nation and I could indeed have changed the world.

Unknown monk, 1100

'Vision is the art of seeing things invisible.'

Jonathan Swift

The President of the Coca Cola Company between 1922 and 1955 had this vision; that no one on the face of the earth should die without having tasted Coca Cola.

'Whoever it was who searched the heavens with a telescope and found no God would not have found the human mind if they had searched the brain with a microscope.'

George Santayana

Visiting

A pastor went visiting one afternoon. He knocked on a door several times, but no one answered. He could see through the window that the TV was on, so he took one of his cards and wrote 'Rev. 3:20 — Behold I stand at the door and knock: if anyone will open I will come in' on it and stuck it in the door.

The following Sabbath, a woman handed him a card with her name on it and the following message, 'Gen. 3:20 — I heard thy voice, and I was naked — so I hid myself.'

Weaknesses

A member of an official board undergoing the process of appointing a new pastor finally lost patience. He'd just witnessed the Pastoral Relations Committee reject applicant after applicant for some minor fault — real or imagined. It was time for a bit of soul-searching on the part of the committee. So he stood up and read this letter purporting to be from another applicant.

Gentlemen: Understanding your pulpit is vacant, I should like to apply for the position. I have many qualifications. I've been a preacher with much success and also had some success as a writer. Some say I'm a good organiser. I've been a leader most places I've been.

I'm over fifty years of age and have never preached in one place for more than three years. In some places I have left town after my work caused riots and disturbances. I must admit I have been in jail three or four times, but not because of any real wrongdoing.

My health is not too good, though I still accomplish a great deal. The churches I have preached in have been small, though located in several large cities.

I've not gotten along well with religious leaders in the towns where I have preached. In fact, some have threatened me, and even attacked me physically. I am not too good at keeping records. I have been known to forget whom I have baptised.

However, if you can use me, I promise to do my best for you.

The board member turned to the committee and said, 'Well, what do you think? Shall we call him?'

The good church folks were appalled! Consider a sickly, trouble-making, absent-minded ex-jailbird? Was the board member crazy? Who signed the application? Who had such colossal nerve?

The board member eyed them all keenly before he replied, 'It's signed, "The Apostle Paul."'

Anon.

The following is a confidential report on several candidates being considered for the ministry.

Noah: Former pastorate of 120 years with not even one convert. Prone to unrealistic building projects.

Joseph: A big thinker, but a braggart; believes in dream-interpreting, and has a prison record.

Moses: A modest and meek man, but poor communicator, even stuttering at times. Sometimes blows his top and acts rashly. Some say he left an earlier church over a murder charge.

David: The most promising leader of all until we discovered the affair he had with his neighbour's wife.

Solomon: Great preacher but our parsonage would never hold all those wives.

Elijah: Prone to depression. Collapses under pressure.

Elisha: Reported to have lived with a single widow while at his former church.

Hosea: A tender and loving pastor but our people could never handle his wife's occupation.

Jeremiah: Emotionally unstable, alarmist, negative, always lamenting things, reported to have taken a long trip to bury his underwear on the bank of a foreign river.

Isaiah: On the fringe? Claims to have seen angels in church. Has trouble with his language.

Melchizedek: Great credentials at current work place, but where does this guy come from? No information in his CV about former work records. Every line about parents was left blank and he refused to supply a birth date.

John: Says he is a Baptist, but definitely doesn't dress like one. Has slept in the outdoors for months on end, has a weird diet, and provokes denominational leaders.

God doesn't call the equipped, he equips the called.

Anon.

If you ever feel unworthy, you're in good company:

Moses stuttered.
David's armour didn't fit.
John Mark was rejected by Paul.
Timothy had ulcers.
Hosea's wife was a prostitute.
Amos' only training was in the school of fig-tree pruning.
Jacob was a liar.
David had an affair.
Solomon was too rich.
Jesus was too poor.
Abraham was too old.
David was too young.
Peter was afraid of death.
Lazarus was dead.
John was self-righteous.
Naomi was a widow.
Paul was a murderer.
So was Moses.
Jonah ran from God.
Miriam was a gossip.
Gideon and Thomas both doubted.
Jeremiah was a depressive.
Elijah was burned out.
John the Baptist was a loudmouth.
Martha was a worrier.
Her sister may have been lazy.
Samson had long hair.
Noah got drunk.
Did I mention that Moses had a short fuse?
So did Peter, Paul — well, lots of people did.

But God doesn't require a job interview. He doesn't hire and fire like most bosses, because he's more our dad than our boss. He doesn't look at financial gain or loss. He's not prejudiced or partial, not judging, grudging, not deaf to our cry, not blind to our need. As much as we try, God's gifts are free.

Anon.

Wealth

John Paul Getty was the richest man in the world, he was worth over 4 billion dollars, which is a considerable amount of money and this is what he said:

'I have never been given to envy except for the envy I feel towards those folk who have the ability to make a marriage work and be happy in that marriage.'

He said, 'It's an art I have never been able to master. My record — five marriages, five divorces, in short, five failures, I have never been happy.'

Alexander the Great inherited one empire and conquered another. He literally bought the East and the West. He had all of this by the age of thirty-three. He quickly became disillusioned with life because of all that he had, much like Solomon, understanding that possessions could not bring happiness. He had enough presence of mind to request that when he died he would have his hands open, so that people who came to view his body would realise that the man who owned the whole world left with nothing.

Words

Here are some actual label instructions on consumer goods:

On Tesco's tiramisu dessert (printed on bottom of the box): Do not turn upside down.

On Marks and Spencer's bread pudding:
Product will be hot after heating.

On packaging for a Rowenta iron:
Do not iron clothes on body.

On Boot's children's cough medicine: Do not drive car or operate machinery.

On Nytol sleep aid:
Warning: may cause drowsiness.

On a Korean kitchen knife:
Warning: keep out of children.

On a string of Chinese-made Christmas lights: For indoor or outdoor use only.

On Sainsbury's peanuts:
Warning: contains nuts.

On a Swedish chainsaw:
Do not attempt to stop chain with your hands.

On a child's superman costume: Wearing of this garment does not enable you to fly.

Worry

Said the robin to the sparrow:
'I should really like to know
Why these anxious human beings
Rush about and worry so.'

Said the sparrow to the robin:
'Friend I think that it must be
That they have no heavenly Father
Such as cares for you and me.'

Anon.

Never let yesterday use up too much of today.

Worry does not empty tomorrow of its sorrow, it empties today of its strength.
Corrie Ten Boom

'When I look at the world I get distressed. When I look at myself I get depressed. But when I look at Jesus, I find rest.'
Corrie Ten Boom

'If I spent as much time doing the things I worry about getting done as I do worrying about them, I wouldn't have anything to worry about.'
Beryl Pfizer

'**Half the worry in the world is caused by people trying to make decisions before they have sufficient knowledge on which to base a decision.**'
Dean Hawkes

Worship

Worship is our response to the overtures of love from the heart of the Father.
Richard Foster

An old farmer went to the city one weekend and attended the big city church. He came home and his wife asked him how it was.

'Well,' said the farmer, 'It was good. They did something different, however. They sang praise choruses instead of hymns.'

'Praise choruses,' said his wife, 'What are those?'

'Oh, they're OK. They're sort of like hymns, only different,' said the farmer.

'Well, what's the difference?' asked his wife.

The farmer said, 'Well it's like this — If I were to say to you: "Martha, the cows are in the corn," well that would be a hymn. If, on the other hand, I were to say to you: "Martha Martha, Martha, Oh, Martha, MARTHA, MARTHA, the cows, the big cows, the brown cows, the black cows, the white cows, the black-and-white cows, the COWS, COWS, COWS are in the corn, are in the corn, are in the corn, are in the corn, the CORN, CORN, CORN." Then, if I were to repeat the whole thing two or three times, well that would be a praise chorus.'

Now, the rebuttal, so to speak:

A young, new Christian went to his local church usually, but one weekend attended a small town church. He came home and his wife asked him how it was.

'Well,' said the young man, 'It was good. They did something different, however. They sang hymns instead of the usual songs.'

'Hymns,' said his wife, 'What are those?'

'Oh, they're OK. They're sort of like songs, only different,' said the young man.

'Well, what's the difference?' asked his wife.

The young man said, 'Well, it's like this — If I were to say to you, "Martha, the cows are in the corn," well, that would be a song. If, on the other hand, I were to say to you:

Oh Martha, dear Martha, hear thou my cry
Inclinest thine ear to the words of my mouth.
Turn thou thy whole wondrous ear by and by
To the righteous, inimitable, glorious truth.

For the way of the animals who can explain?
There in their heads is no shadow of sense,
Hearkenest they in God's sun or his rain
Unless from the mild, tempting corn they are fenced.

Yea those cows in glad bovine, rebellious delight,
Have broke free their shackles, their warm pens eschewed.
Then goaded by minions of darkness and night
They all my mild Chilliwack sweet corn have chewed.

So look to that bright shining day by and by,
Where all foul corruptions of earth are reborn.
Where no vicious animal makes my soul cry
And I no longer see those foul cows in the corn.

'Then, if I were to do only verses one, three and four and do a key change on the last verse, well that would be a hymn.'

Anon.

Worth

A well known speaker started off his seminar by holding up a £50 note.

In the room of 200, he asked, 'Who would like this £50 note?' Hands started going up. He said, 'I am going to give it to one of you, but first let me do this.'

He proceeded to crumple the note up. He then asked, 'Who still wants it?'

Still the hands were up in the air.

'Well,' he replied, 'what if I do this?' And he dropped it on the ground and started to grind it into the floor with his shoe. He picked it up, now all crumpled and dirty.

'Now who still wants it?' Still the hands went into the air.

'My friends, you have all learned a very valuable lesson. No matter what I did to the money, you still wanted it because it did not decrease in value. It was still worth £50.'

Many times in our lives, we are dropped, crumpled and ground into the dirt by the decisions we make and the circumstances that come our way. We feel as though we are worthless. But no matter what has happened or what will happen, you will never lose your value in God's eyes. To him, dirty or clean, crumpled or finely creased, you are still priceless to him.

X Files

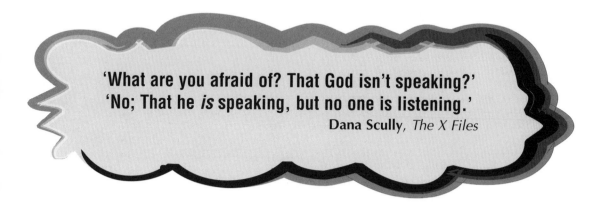

'What are you afraid of? That God isn't speaking?'
'No; That he *is* speaking, but no one is listening.'

Dana Scully, *The X Files*

> *I'm a non-religious person in*
> *search of a religious experience.*
> **Chris Carter**, creator of *The X Files*

Youth

The girl's prayer

Our Marks
Which art with Spencers
Hallowed be thy food-hall
Thy Gucci watch
Thy Kookai bag
In Hermes
As it is in Harrods
Give us each day our Visa Gold
And forgive us our overdraft
As we forgive those who stop our
    Next card
And lead us not into Dorothy
    Perkins
And deliver us from Top Shop
For thine is the Naff Naff, the
    Cartier and the Versace
For Gaultier and Eternity
AMEX

Anon.

The lad's prayer

Our beer
Which art in barrels
Hallowed be thy drink
Thy will be drunk
I will be drunk
At home as it is in the local
Forgive us this day our daily
    spillage
As we forgive those who spillest
    against us
And lead us not into the practice of
    poncey wine-tasting
And deliver us from alco-pops
For mine is the bitter
The ale and the lager
For ever and ever
BARMEN

Anon.

Before going on holiday, we wrote down some instructions for the person who was to look after our guinea pigs. After reading through our instructions once again, I noticed similarities with the care of teenagers:

- Please fill up their bowls with food each morning, and make sure they have a drink.
- In the evening give them fruit and vegetables.
- Clear out any uneaten food from their quarters each day.
- Only let them out if you think it is safe as they are shy, but some like cuddles and all of them love being pampered.
- Protect from too much sun or cold nights.
- They each need some time on their own, girls live in groups of two or more.
- Separate boys and girls after six weeks.

Jo and Karen Stephens

In Bill Gates' new book, he lays out eleven rules that students do not learn in high school or college, but should. He argues that our feel-good, politically correct teachings have created a generation of children with no concept of reality who are set up for failure in the real world.

The list:

Rule 1. Life is not fair; get used to it.

Rule 2. The world won't care about your self-esteem. The world will expect you to accomplish something *before* you feel good about yourself.

Rule 3. You will *not* make $40,000 a year right out of high school. You won't be a vice president with a car phone until you earn both.

Rule 4. If you think your teacher is tough, wait till you get a boss. He doesn't have tenure.

Rule 5. Flipping burgers is not beneath your dignity. Your grandparents had a different word for burger-flipping; they called it opportunity.

Rule 6. If you mess up, it's not your parents' fault, so don't whine about your mistakes, learn from them.

Rule 7. Before you were born, your parents weren't as boring as they are now. They got that way from paying your bills, cleaning your clothes and listening to you talk about how cool you are. So before you save the rain forest from the parasites of your parents' generation, try 'delousing' the closet in your own room.

Rule 8. Your school may have done away with winners and losers, but life has not. In some schools they have abolished failing grades; they'll give you as many times as you want to get the right answer. This doesn't bear the slightest resemblance to *anything* in real life.

Rule 9. Life is not divided into semesters. You don't get summers off and very few employers are interested in helping you find yourself. Do that in your own time.

Rule 10. Television is *not* real life. In real life people actually have to leave the coffee shop and go to jobs.

Rule 11. Be nice to nerds. Chances are you'll end up working for one.

The new school prayer

Now I sit me down in school
Where praying is against the rule
For this great nation under God
Finds mention of Him very odd.
If Scripture now the class recites,
It violates the Bill of Rights.
And anytime my head I bow
Becomes a Federal matter now.
Our hair can be purple, orange or green,
That's no offence; it's a freedom scene.
The law is specific, the law is precise.
Prayers spoken aloud are a serious vice.
For praying in a public hall
Might offend someone with no faith at all.
In silence alone we must meditate,
God's name is prohibited by the state.
We're allowed to cuss and dress like freaks,
And pierce our noses, tongues and cheeks.
They've outlawed guns, but FIRST the Bible.
To quote the Good Book makes me liable.
We can elect a pregnant Senior Queen,
And the 'unwed daddy,' our Senior King.
It's 'inappropriate' to teach right from wrong,
We're taught that such 'judgements' do not belong.
We can get our condoms and birth controls,
Study witchcraft, vampires and totem poles.
But the Ten Commandments are not allowed,
It's scary here I must confess,
When chaos reigns the school's a mess.
So, Lord, this silent plea I make:
Should I be shot; my soul please take!
Amen.

Written by a teenager in Bagdad, Arizona, USA.

A message from one generation to another:

We trusted you to live healthy lives before our conception; you
    abused yourselves with abnormal sex, drugs and nicotine.
We trusted you for nourishment; you fed us contamination.
We trusted you to keep our bodies pure; you made us addicts.
We trusted you with our safety; you passed laws to abort our lives.
We trusted you with our future; you gave us AIDS.
We trusted you for love and affection; you left us abandoned.
We trusted you for a healthy diet; you cop out with junk food.
We trusted you for our moral guidance; you set a pathetic example.
We trusted you with our spiritual well-being; you never even
    mention Jesus.
We trusted you with our education; yet you let our schools fall
    apart.
We trusted you to keep our eyes pure; you make explicit films of
    sex and violence.
We trusted you to keep our ears pure; you swear and blaspheme in
    front of us.
We trusted you to keep our mouths pure; you feed us obscene
    literature and songs to recite.
We trusted you with our hearts so young; you encourage us to grow
    old before our time.
We trusted you with our mental welfare; you screwed up our minds
    with your double standards.
We trusted you on building relationships; you locked us away
    inside video games.
We trusted you to show us truth; you gave us virtual reality.
We trusted you for family values; you gave us common-law
    partners.
We trusted you for our innocence; you abused our bodies.
We trusted you with our adolescence; you encourage safe sex and
    contraception.
We trusted you for what's right and wrong; you mock what's right
    and defend what's wrong.
We trusted you with the whole of our future; what future?
We trusted you...!

The worst danger that confronts the younger generation is the example set by the older generation.

It seems a lot of young people want an occupation that doesn't keep them occupied.

A misspent youth may result in a tragic old age.

It must be wonderful to be young enough to know everything.

Zeal

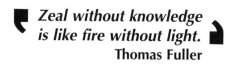 *Zeal without knowledge
is like fire without light.*
Thomas Fuller